Press

Divine GASHUGI

BAREFOOT IN GERMANY

Novel

Cover designer: Wistitruck

Editor: Leah Dunlevy

Layout: Jette Loeper

1

My family lived in Kigali, the capital city of Rwanda in the heart of Africa.

Our house was located behind Nyamirambo market, a neighborhood that smelled of raw fish by the time the sun rose.

The evening wind scattered the greasy scents of Chapati and Samosa, which were deep fried on charcoal stoves and sold on every street corner. Despite growing up in that quarter of Nyamirambo, there was one thing I never managed to learn: being able to differentiate the flies coming out of our latrine from the ones flying around the market (or maybe there was no difference between them after all).

Like my peers, I was dreaming about getting the best job in Rwanda. I wanted to become the first person in my family to own a car. I talked about moving into an apartment in Kiyovu, the fanciest neighborhood in Kigali, and of course, marrying the love of my life.

When reality harshly revealed itself to me, I wished I could have known that dreaming is free for all, but very few will actually pay the price it costs to turn their dreams into reality. None of my childhood dreams came true and it seemed as though I would have to wait a lifetime.

Most of my former classmates have married, acquired stable jobs, or moved abroad. I was stuck in the same place, with only my Bachelor's degree and no hope for the future. *Ese uzaduha inzoga ryari?* When will you offer us drinks? Everyone asked me. That's an indirect way of asking, "When are you getting married?" A typical question Rwandans would ask a 23-year-old girl who didn't introduce a fiancé or talk about marriage plans.

Social pressure constructed marriage into an achievement for girls and served as an escape from financial responsibilities.

I had graduated from university a year ago, and I was still busy sending my résumé everywhere hoping that, at least one day, I would get that coveted invitation to a job interview. But after my mother's death, life took a different direction.

As for my father, apart from knowing that he was the man who used his wealth to find his way between the thighs of vulnerable girls, I didn't have any memory of him. I lived as if he had never existed. My father, John Musonera, had met mama when she was only 18, on her way to APACE where she attended secondary school. He stopped his Rav4 too close to her, as if he was about to drive over her feet.

"Do you want a ride?" He asked, scanning her silhouette.

"No thanks, my school is there," she pointed at a building a few meters ahead.

"Come on, I can still drive you there. It's not like my car seats have thorns that could hurt your beautiful body," he smiled.

She reluctantly accepted his offer. She quickly climbed into his car and stared outside of the car window.

"So, what's your name? Mine is John, but you can call me Jo." He used his palm to pull her face towards him.

"Please drive or I'll get out and walk. I can't be late," she said, removing his hand from her cheek.

"Okay, but only if you tell me your name."

"Nirere Speciose. I prefer to be called Nirere. Now, could you please drive or open the door and let me walk?"

He drove very slowly while singing along to the jingle that was playing on the radio.

"Imodoka zubu zaranyobeye ugenda mu muhanda ikaguhitana, wayihungira kure, ikagusanga yo."

He parked behind the school building and pulled his wallet out of his pocket before he opened the door for her to get out.

"This is for you," he said, handing her 5000 Rwandan francs. "Maybe you can take a taxi or motorbike back home. I hate to see a pretty girl like you walking on these dusty roads. You should move into a better neighborhood like Kacyiru or Kiyovu."

"Thank you, sir…John, Jo, I mean," she stuttered. "Thank you very much. You have no idea how much I was in need for money. May God bless you."

"Look, we can talk later, and see how I can take care of you. Of course, you need to be taken care of," Jo said, seeing her elation. He caressed her thigh up and down.

"I didn't know kind people still exist. Thank you very much John," she replied.

"Please, call me Jo." He pulled out a piece of paper, scribbled something on it and handed it over. "This is my number, call me when you want to discuss about how I can support you. Okay?"

"I will call you today after school. I promise."

He opened the door for her to leave the car and said, "Oh you know what, there is a bar around here that roasts chicken and fish very good, we can go to eat there later."

Chicken? Fish? That was food mama had never fantasized about eating because she could never afford it. It was for those children who had rich parents. She pushed her 5000 francs in her blue uniform skirt and tucked in her white shirt just as the headmaster insisted the students should dress, and then entered the school building.

As soon as mama left class that day, she rushed to the public phone *Tuvugane* and informed John that she was free. He was at customs, solving issues about the goods he had imported from China. He told her to go home and instructed her to meet him in the evening at the Green Corner bar.

Mama spent the afternoon singing while she polished her shoes and ironed her best blouse with a charcoal iron that she, for the first time, had borrowed from Mama Amina.

That evening at Green Corner, mama told John about how she lived alone and thanks to the Muslim community of Nyamirambo, she could go to school and have a meal twice a day. John listened without interrupting her. He nodded his head as he slowly sipped from his Primus that occasionally left foam on his mustache. Mama told him about how she had lost her whole family during the Genocide against Tutsi in 1994, and she was the only one among her eight siblings who survived. John rubbed his hands against each other, stared to the side and turned to look into her eyes that were, by then, full of tears.

"Don't cry. You have found me now, okay." He held her hands in his softly. "So, here is a suggestion," he continued, "Call me whenever you feel lonely and I'll come to give you company. Whenever you are hungry, when you have any problem, especially financial problems, I will help you."

Mama stared at his wedding ring, unsure whether to ask if he was talking about friendship, parenting, or just supporting a poor girl. Instead she said, "Thank you very much."

"Now come closer," John said, pulling her against himself. He slid his hand towards her breasts, while another firmly held her shoulders.

"What are you doing?" She pushed him away and moved back to where she was sitting before.

"Look, I can take care of all your needs. Any need. But you will also have to take care of mine," he winked.

"But you are married, aren't you?" She looked into his eyes.

"So what?" He asked her mockingly, raising his eyebrows.

"Are you going to tell your wife?"

"Oh dear, no wonder why you remain poor despite your beauty." He moved closer to her, too close that the smell of Primus beer from his mouth suffocated her, and she worried she would end up drunk even though she had only drank two bottles of Sprite. "Leave my wife out of our arrangement. It will just be between us, okay? Do you think all of your classmates who wear nice shoes, carry bags that you envy, or come to school on motorbikes all have rich parents? No, some of them are lucky to fall on a man like me. Look, this is an offer, not an obligation. So, you are free to choose between your current life and the one you'd like to have." He leaned back, letting her think about his offer.

In the months that followed, they met a few times in hotels and guesthouses. He paid her rent and bought her everything that, at her age, she needed and wanted. Fancy second hand clothes, a watch, and her first Nokia mobile phone that the neighbors called "*Mobayilo*" whenever they borrowed it to call their relatives. Like many other married men, John complained about the changes on his wife's body and that she wasn't giving him enough attention after she gave birth. He was looking for adventure— something that he didn't think was available at home. He began taking Nirere to Lake Kivu on the weekends and he introduced her to night clubs where she would occasionally drink alcohol.

A few months later, as they both enjoyed the life of their mutual agreement, Nirere told John that she was pregnant. They were laying next to each other in Muhabura Hotel, sweat covering their bodies from the action they had just finished.

"What? How could you be so stupid? You know I have a wife and two children. I don't need more," he answered while jumping out of bed as if an aggressive animal was about to attack him.

"But I didn't know. You should have warned me," she started crying while John hurried to wear his trousers.

"Who knew then? Or what is it that you didn't know?"

"I didn't know that I would get pregnant if you kept refusing to use condoms."

"Nonsense." He fastened the last button of his shirt and came closer to the bed. "Did I ever force you?" She shook her head. "Were you not happy accepting my money and spending it on whatever crossed your mind?" She nodded yes. "So why didn't you also buy pills or anything else that would have protected you from pregnancy?"

She cried.

He put on his shoes.

She cleaned her nose and wiped the tears from her face.

"Are you leaving that bed or do you want me to buy you this hotel room as well?" John scoffed.

She sat up straight in bed. "So what are we doing?"

He turned to her. "We? Who are we? Am I pregnant? Go sort it out as soon as possible. There are some doctors in private clinics who are specialized in that, so do your research and let me know how much you need."

"Do you mean abortion?"

"Mhm," he answered.

"No, I cannot. What if I die while doing it? I had a classmate who died last year. Trust me, it's very risky."

"Then it's up to you to decide. Pregnancy wasn't part of what we agreed on. After all, it's your body, so do whatever you want but as I said I don't need any baby," he moved to stand next to the door. "I will wait for you in the car. Hurry up and I will drop you to your house. I have a business to run."

Nirere never saw John again, and whenever she called his number he didn't pick up. Her belly grew big and she was kicked out of school to deal with everything on her own. The women from Muslim communities supported her during birth and were there to help after I was born. John sent her an envelope full of money with a handwritten note saying that he wanted nothing to do with the child. And with that, she never heard from him again. The neighbors advised her to take him to court using that note he wrote as a proof. But who was he? She would take him to court and then what? How could she be sure that John Musonera was his real name since other people they ran into would call him different names? She used his money to open a small kiosk, which she later developed into a restaurant.

Tears fell from mama's eyes as she told me about my father. It was the day after my fifteenth birthday. The rain violently pounded the roof as we sat together in the kitchen peeling potatoes.

"I will fight for you, even if it means losing my life. You will go to school and study, and you will go far. I promise you. Your life will never be anything like mine," she cried while hugging me tight.

"Thanks mama," I released myself from her arms and continued peeling potatoes.

"Until my last breath. I promise you," she slid her index finger around her neck, swearing, "I will offer you the best education. The key to success."

2

Living in a society that considered depression an imaginary western sickness, I received no professional help to overcome the loss of my mother.

Pole and *wihangane* were the words that I heard from neighbors and friends. Whenever my sister Tendeza left the house, I didn't know when and if she would come back alive. Neighbors used to gossip that they saw her with men at Kosmos near the stadium, an area that was infamous for sexually transmitted diseases. Yes, I wanted to help my sister. But I didn't know how. Our house had lost the meaning of home and became simply the building where we met to sleep or fight. Poverty welcomed itself into our family and even eating twice a day had become a privilege.

Unlike me, Tendeza looked exactly like mama: big round eyes that always had a soft look even when she was full of anger and a thin nose that saved her from the drama of being asked if she was Hutu or Tutsi. Her tall height made people think she was older than me. The only thing I inherited from mama was her smile and her naiveté that allowed her to easily trust people.

Tendeza's father, Abdul, was the driver of the bus that had the hip hop artist 50 Cent painted on it. Years ago, everyone who was cool in Kigali tried to ride this bus before painting celebrities on Nyamirambo-City-center buses became common. Abdul died in a car accident when Tendeza was five years old. He had never lived with us because he wasn't yet ready to start a family, but he would visit us sometimes.

Five months after mama's death, I posted on my Facebook, "I want to disappear from this world." This post brought me many sympathetic comments. Amongst people who commented on my post was Sonia Mukamana, a former classmate and neighbor, who moved to Dubai when we finished high school. A few years had passed without hearing any news from Sonia, and then suddenly she appeared on Facebook. Her Facebook account said that she lived in Hamburg, Germany. I started chatting with Sonia from time to time on Facebook and I liked all her photos, which showed her living what looked to me like the best life. To be honest, I envied her. She was always posing with fancy cars, in restaurants, and in front of big buildings.

Sonia, who used to be as dark as asphalt road had turned herself into *Muzungu*. She wore long straightened wigs and bright makeup on her whitened skin.

Sonia commented on my post: "Yoo pole my dear Toni. Let me know if I can help."

I immediately messaged her, "*Sha uzampe passe y'umuzungu.*" Straight to the point, I asked her to find me a white man. I wanted a rich charming prince who would take me away from my responsibilities. When Sonia replied to me, she asked the characteristics of a man I would like. Instead of wasting time inventing one of those ideal men that exist only in the minds of young women, I explained to her that I would accept anybody. Even if she found a man the age of my father, no problem. Age is, after all, just a number. Isn't it?

Rumors spread in Nyamirambo, some said that Sonia washed dead bodies for a living. Others said that she was a prostitute there. It was impossible to know what to believe from our neighbors; they were gossips who would talk from Monday to Sunday. Sonia had told me that she was a hotel receptionist in Dubai but later moved to Germany. How she arrived and what she did there remained a mystery because, as far as I was concerned, even her parents didn't know. Or maybe, they never asked. She sent money to her family, supported her parents financially to build a house in Kicukiro, and opened a wedding decorating business for her mother. Sonia's father bragged about how his daughter had become rich in Europe. But who cares about knowing the details of people who live in Europe? They are all busy, anyway. I knew from her mother that she worked a lot, and I assumed that she would have no time to answer me.

3

Tendeza came to sit next to me while I cleaned my shoes with an old toothbrush. "You know what Toni," she said. My full name is Mutoni but people called me Toni and I liked the nickname.

"What?" I turned to look at her.

"I am going to Dubai," she said with a bright smile on her face.

Dubai was the place most girls of our generation sought while boys went to Darfur or Mozambique. I have heard stories of boys who went to Mozambique and that they became successful traders. Some of them came back home to marry and took their wives with them. Boys who went to Darfur returned with enough money to build houses and start their own businesses. Nobody talked about the ones who lost their lives abroad. Now my little sister was also leaving to chase fortune on her own.

"And how are you going to Dubai?" I asked Tendeza.

"You should first say something like congratulations, or I am proud of you."

"Oh well, I don't know if you are not making a mistake."

Tendeza quickly became upset. "Will you ever stop nagging? I can't be you, Mutoni, nor will I ever do everything you expect from me. So stop behaving as if you are my mother."

"It's alright. You don't have to yell. So how are you going to Dubai?"

"Haruna is taking me there. He found me a job as a hotel receptionist."

Haruna was the only man I disliked among the clients who frequented the restaurant where worked weekends and any extra shifts. That small restaurant is what you would call a kiosk but was considered a restaurant in Nyamirambo. We sold samosas, chapati and refreshing drinks as the sign on the door read: *Amata na Fanta bikonje.*

Haruna wore a heavy silver necklace that rested on his belly, which was as big as an overripe pregnancy. One evening while paying for his meal, he leaned close to me, so close that I could smell that he oiled his skin with *Tajiri*. "You are too beautiful to work here," he said.

"Thanks, but beauty has nothing to do with food," I shrugged.

"Look, I can find you a job anywhere in this country," he whispered in my ear. I was immediately uncomfortable.

"Really?" I mocked him, but he understood it as an honest question.

"I have connections, you know. Let's discuss about this opportunity after you close the restaurant. I can wait for you somewhere else," he said.

"Alright, give me your number and I will call you when I close."

I thought maybe he could get me a job at the community bank. He seemed to know many people, that was true. Later I called him and we met at Amani Lodge. He began by rubbing my back and insisted that since our conversation is very confidential, we should discuss in his room. He moved his hands down to grab my butt. I slapped them away and I understood what he wanted from me. I took a motorbike taxi and immediately went home crying. That night I hated myself for being so naïve. Before going to meet him, I should have been skeptical about the kind of connections he had that didn't give him a job himself. But I didn't tell Tendeza anything.

I couldn't allow my sister to fall into Haruna's trap. I worried about what may have happened when they discussed Tendeza's supposed Dubai adventure. What would happen to her if he ever takes her there?

"Haruna is a monster. He will ruin your life," I said.

"More than it's ruined now?" Tendeza answered mockingly. "Look at us, what do we have?"

"You are still young Tendeza. You could even go back to study."

"Studying, studying…and then what? Then become like you?"

"I am sorry," I pulled her into my arms while tears ran down my cheeks.

"It's just that when I think of how mother tried her best to make sure we studied, it would make her proud if you went back. And maybe I could even find you a scholarship for continuing abroad later," I said.

"And you really think that it's my responsibility to make dead people proud? You know what the problem is here?" She released herself from my arms. "Everyone wants to gain higher education but they won't find where to apply for it, and while doing that, they miss other opportunities."

"Well, at least I am educated."

"Yes, you have academic education but you lack in street smarts," she said.

"You are just looking for excuses for your ignorance, Tendeza."

"So you are calling me ignorant? Watch me."

Tendeza shifted her attention to her phone and began scrolling up and down.

A heavy silence hung between us.

I stood up to put my shoes on the window where they were drying overnight, and I asked Tendeza, "So when are you planning to leave?"

"Tomorrow evening. I already have everything ready."

"What?"

Before I could control myself, a slap escaped me and landed on my sister's face. "Are you sick? When were you going to tell me about this?"

"I hate you. If this is what you call being a caring sister then I don't want to see you again in my life," she shouted.

I cried before her "I am sorry, I really want…"

"Save your excuses for your miserable life." She shrugged me off as I tried to hold her hand. "Leave me alone." She went to bed without another word.

That night I slept in the living room on the sofa.

The next day I woke up very early and ran to a neighborhood shop to buy donuts and eggs. I cooked porridge and fried eggs and set up the breakfast table.

At the very least, I wanted to share a last meal with my sister before she left. I had prepared the sentence I would use to apologize for last night's incident. "My dear sister, I understand that each one of us has our own life to live. I hope you find happiness in whatever you choose. Count on me if you ever need help."

I waited and waited in the living room but Tendeza didn't come out of the sleeping room.

A strange feeling of worry made me knock on the door, but nobody answered. I pushed the door to find that Tendeza was not there and the suitcase she had next to the bed was gone. On the pillow lay a note: "I left so that you could make your parenting advice useful for yourself. I will write you on Whatsapp soon with my Dubai number."

I practiced breathing in and out deeply. I forced my mind to believe that I was dreaming, but I couldn't deny the reality.

What have I done in life?

I cried.

What have I done to people that I love?

Why me?

I went to lay under the mango tree in our compound and got lost in my thoughts. I didn't mind the hot sun; I was pleased to be there alone.

There was no answer to my questions, except life teaching me that I was growing up. I didn't know how long I laid there— maybe an hour or two. I closed my eyes and tried so hard to think of one reason to stay in Rwanda. There was none.

4

At school I wasn't the girl who would enter the room and make heads turn. And I never would be.

I remember how the bullies used to call me *Rutwe,* referring to my big round head on a petite body. But when Sonia sent me a photo of her rich German friend who was mesmerized by my photos, I snapped out of my victimized mindset. After all, living in Europe meant becoming rich, smelling very good, and above all, being called "Diaspora" when I would come back home to visit. Diaspora was a name that earned you respect in Rwanda. A name that brought you closer to uncles or aunties you had never heard about before and a name that made Rwandan suitors accept your hand in marriage without *Gusaba, Gukwa* and an elaborate church ceremony.

Accepting Sonia's offer of moving to Germany to meet the man she had found for me was the best decision I could make. At least that's what I thought when I made that decision. Why not? Kabibi was in

Oman, Natasha was in Mozambique and Shema was getting ready to go to France next week. What was left to lose, anyway? I reasoned that if I went to Germany with my degree in marketing I would even have a better life than Sonia. I was an educated woman. I wrote Sonia and explained to her that I would love to meet her friend Sebastian. I said that I would be ready to leave Rwanda as soon as possible.

The next day, after reading Sonia's answer to my message, I simply replied to her that I agreed to everything. She called me on Skype so that I could talk to Sebastian. His effortless smile and his blue eyes, vibrant even through the camera, made me feel like I had met him somewhere before, maybe in my dreams. We had a short, almost non-verbal conversation.

"How are you?" He said.

"I am fine, and you?" I said smiling.

"All good. Sonia said that you want to come here. That's nice."

"Yes, I want to come as soon as possible," I said.

He glanced at his watch, ran his hand through his brown golden hair and excused himself, saying that he had to leave. He had an important meeting, so he said that Sonia would organize my trip and answer all questions I may have.

That day I went to knock on the door of Mama Joy. She was our mother's favorite neighbor and friend. After mother passed away, she was the only person who was there for us, so I felt the need to inform her about the good news. Her house always had loud Ugandan music on.

"Toni, *ni amahoro?*" Is everything okay? That was how she greeted me as she opened the door and pulled me inside. Her Kitenge wrapper hung loosely around her chest, as if pulling it tighter would prevent oxygen from circulating in her body.

"Yes Aunty, all is well; I am moving to Europe," I said.

She shook her head like someone waking up from a dream and looked at me. "*Iburayi?*"

"Yes, I have received a scholarship to get my masters at a German university and I will also work there," I lied to her with confidence.

"*Reka sha, mbwira neza.*" Come closer and explain to me properly, she said, smiling and pulling me in her arms.

We sat on her bed, since her house consisted of one room. Mama Joy listened to me with excitement. I talked about how Sonia had found me a university in Germany where I would be able to study and get my masters in two years. I lied about a cousin of Sonia who was the director of an international trading company, saying he was willing to hire me as his assistant. I explained how the university would even take care of anything related to my visa application and pay my travel costs. Mama Joy said, "Wow, *wabona uzanarongorwa n'umuzungu.*" Probably you will even marry a white man.

However, Mama Joy was a little skeptical about Sonia.

"But I heard stories that Sonia is *malaya* in Dubai," she said.

"A prostitute?" I asked.

"Hum, they talked about her in Karibu Hair Saloon when I was getting these cornrows done," she ran her hand through her hair.

I explained to her that Dubai is not Germany, that now we were talking about Europe, where she lives.

"Aunty, Europe. *Iburayi*," I said, looking into her eyes to ensure she understood that it was not Africa we were discussing.

"Yes, of course I know Germany. The country that won the world cup in football. Right?"

"That was a few years ago." We laughed. Mama Joy had a deep voice and a strong, scratchy laugh.

With a serious look I asked her, "But Aunty, do you really care about what Sonia has done in Dubai if she managed to move to Europe afterwards? Look how she is changing her mother's life, uhm."

She tightened her wrapper and looked at me. "Well, I would only advise you to be careful. People around here gossip a lot, so you never know what is true or false.

When you get there, just focus on your studies. Don't get distracted."

I added that even if she was a *malaya* in Germany, it didn't mean that I would be working with her. I had my diploma and I was an educated girl.

"Come here my girl," she said while hugging me so tight that I was scared my ribs would break into pieces, "Kneel down and we thank God."

I released myself from her arms and then pretended that I had just remembered, "Oh by the way, Aunty, Tendeza went to Dubai. She found a job as a hotel receptionist there."

Mama Joy raised up both arms as if trying to touch the ceiling then bent to touch the ground instead. "Blessings over blessings. God is good my daughter. He answers at the right time."

We said a short prayer and I left.

A few days later, Sonia sent me all of the documents I needed from Sebastian for my visa application. I put all of the requirements together and applied for the Schengen visa. The invitation, written by Sebastian

Baumann, explained how we would spend three months together in Hamburg, and travel to Paris, Amsterdam and Venice. They sent me accommodation, travel insurance, a detailed itinerary and proof of financial support.

The biggest excitement of my life was the day when the embassy called me to collect my passport. Weeks before I had to force my legs to move when I first went to apply for the visa. The woman in the glass window who spoke broken Kinyarwanda, mixing it up with English, had looked deep into my eyes after putting my papers into one folder. If a stare could break a human, I would have turned into thousands of pieces that day. "Is that your boyfriend you are going to visit?" she asked.

"Yes, for three months only."

She kept her eyes on me, picked up her water bottle to take a sip and in that moment, I wished I could have the energy to ask for some. Swallowing the little saliva left in my mouth felt like forcing down a piece of boiled cassava.

She looked through my documents once more and said, "Alright, have a nice day. We shall call you if we need any more documents." A heavy weight was lifted from my shoulders as I turned to walk out of the embassy.

Holding my passport with a visa sticker in it that day, I went home, but passed by Kiyovu because I was afraid that my new passport would get stolen if I passed through the city center. Many times, I hesitated to get a motorcycle taxi, afraid that the wind would blow away the whole file and a stranger would pick up my passport. If a stranger saw the visa in there, they would surely ask me for money before giving it back. I checked my passport from time to time, moving it from my handbag to the pocket of my jeans until I decided that holding it in my hands was the safest option. I pinched myself to be sure I was not dreaming. That day I smiled to anybody and anything that crossed my way.

Since Europe meant rich, classy and civilized, I had to train myself.

In order to avoid looking like a real villager when I would arrive in Germany, I slowly started 'Europeanizing' myself, as Mama Joy called it. I was practicing the art of becoming European. I went to the best tailor at Kimironko market and ordered a fitting black suit with a white shirt. The tailor took my measures. I told her that it was very urgent, so she called me to pick it up within three days. Of course I had to pay her a special price. But who cared? I was moving to Europe, so I wasn't worried about spending my savings. My suit made me look like a bank manager or even better, like the female head of the FBI in detective movies.

I had never worn nor owned high heel shoes before but going to Europe was worth the trial. Dressing European was a must. In order to avoid looking ridiculous in the shoes shop because I didn't know how to walk in high heels, I decided to just buy my size without trying them on. I picked the red high heels. The seller insisted that I first try them on to be sure, but I refused. I convinced him that I had exactly the same pair in black, so I knew very well what I was buying. Every evening at home, I practiced cat walking before sleep. Over time, I was getting better.

On Sunday evening Mama Joy rode with me to the airport in a taxi that she had even offered to pay for. As we hugged and said our goodbyes, I removed the sim card from my Samsung, and handed her my phone. "Aunty, this phone will be better than yours, right? Otherwise I won't be able to send you photos of what Europe looks like."

"Oh thank you very much Toni."

"It has Whatsapp— Joy will teach you how to use it. I am sure she knows."

I made her what felt like one hundred promises. I was determined to make it in Europe. I was going to work, study and enjoy life with Sebastian, send Mama Joy money and travel to Dubai to have a good time with my little sister.

I had no idea what was ahead.

5

Arriving in Germany during winter felt like entering a freezer. I wished somebody had warned me.

When I set my feet on German soil, I didn't face the culture shock that people used to talk about— I was too focused on the weather shock instead. My face burned from the cold as if someone had slapped me. I wished they could have told me that the warmest jacket in Kigali would be useless in Hamburg.

A goat taken to the farmer's market in Africa would probably look less frightened than me as I walked out of Hamburg International Airport. I felt lost. And I was, in fact, lost. After two hours of searching for the exit of the airport while struggling in high heels, I had given up and decided to walk barefoot. My legs were shaking, my feet were stinging and I felt paralyzed. Nobody knew me anyway, and the imaginary need for looking classy had made me forget the importance of comfort.

Sonia busted out laughing as soon as she saw me. Who wouldn't laugh at a girl walking barefoot, holding shoes in her hands while being dressed in a beautiful tailor-made suit? "Barefoot, *oya mbabarira winsebya I Burayi,*" Sonia screamed. Barefoot, no please don't make me ashamed in Europe, she said. Did I care? I was disappointed by how other passengers were dressed comfortably while I stumbled in high heels. Sonia hugged me and I noticed that her skin looked like a military uniform. She was white with some dark spots as if the whitening products she used were not effective on every corner of her skin. She was wearing bold red lipstick, a straight blonde wig and high heeled boots. As she hugged me tight, a guy who had been following her grabbed my suitcase. "No, what are you doing?" I pulled back the suitcase. Sonia took my hand off the suitcase, "It's fine, don't worry. He is with us." She pushed her hair away from her face.

Did she have a bodyguard? I wondered for a second but I figured that I would have enough time to get answers for all of my questions.

As we drove, I looked out of the window to see if
Europe was exactly as I had imagined it. I wondered if
Europe was full of men and women in suits, all types of
fancy cars, chic women walking around with little
fluffy-haired dogs and celebrities crossing the streets
holding cups of coffee. At least that's how I saw Europe
in the movies, but maybe Germany was different. I
reasoned that there was no rush; three months was
enough time to explore. The closer we got to the
destination, the stranger and more nervous Sonia
behaved. She became as cold as the weather. The driver
on the other hand, kept glancing at us whenever I spoke
to Sonia in Kinyarwanda. He smiled, showing only his
two front upper teeth, a smile that I'd realize later was
common in Germany.

As I talked about how the airplane taking off felt like
a strong hammer hitting my brain, I could tell Sonia was
disinterested. I talked about how I watched movies one
after another through the flight and that the food in the
airplane was too little and tasted like mud. I described
the tiny toilet. I wondered how the male passengers with
big bellies managed to squeeze themselves through such
tiny doors or if they had extra toilets for them. Still,
Sonia reacted with little interest. I couldn't tell if she

wanted me to stop talking altogether or just change the topic. She insisted that we should speak English, otherwise the driver would feel excluded from our conversation and for Europeans, that is not polite. Same as everywhere in the world when you speak a language that people don't understand, I thought to myself. I wanted to add that but she covered her mouth with one finger, giving me a sign that I should stop talking.

We drove into a big compound with a garden that was filled with dead, gray trees. I later learned that it's normal for most plants in winter to wither and die when it gets very cold, and that they are reborn with new leaves and flowers in the spring. I was tired and hungry, but also excited to meet Sebastian. An Asian woman greeted us with a smile and spoke a few German sentences with the driver. She hugged Sonia and then turned to me.

"Hi, my name is Ligaya, you must be Mutoni," she said, shaking my hand.

"Hi, yes. Nice to meet you," I replied to Ligaya. I turned to whisper to Sonia *"Uyu ni nde?"*

"This is Ligaya," Sonia answered in English, patting Ligaya on the shoulders. Then she added, "For anything you need Ligaya will be here for you. Feel at home and don't worry," Sonia said while glancing to the left and right, avoiding my eyes. Finally, she looked down, pretending to be shy.

Everything happened so fast, and I was frustrated that I didn't get a chance to ask any questions. We walked through the empty corridor with two big mirrors on each side. We entered an empty looking sleeping room that had only a king size bed. Ligaya said that I could rest if I wanted to and she would wake me up when someone came. Who was someone? Where was my future boyfriend Sebastian? What exactly was Ligaya's relationship with Sebastian? Why did the house look like a hotel? Question after question was scrambling in my head. Ligaya left immediately after putting my suitcase next to the empty open wardrobe.

Left alone with Sonia, I asked where Sebastian was, but she didn't answer.

"Uhmm... Sebastian," she said as if she didn't understand me properly. She looked down to check her phone

"Yes, where is Sebastian? When am I meeting him?" I repeated the question.

"Sebastian… actually the thing is…" Sonia lifted her eyes up from her phone, glanced at me and then looked out of the window. I heard a loud aggressive knock on the door, and Sonia became nervous. She hugged me tight and I noticed tears in her eyes. "Sonia, *ni iki*?" I asked her what was wrong. A man's voice called from the corridor, "Sonia. Sonia." She pushed me away. "I have to run otherwise I will be late for work."

I took off my shoes and laid on the bed, staring at the ceiling.

Yes, I had no idea where I was. No, I didn't know if Sonia was coming back after work. I knew almost nothing about the man I was there to meet. I remembered Mama Joy's last words at the airport, "*Ntuzasebere I mahanga ufite iwanyu.*" Don't live a shameful life abroad when you have a home. What exactly did she mean?

Ligaya came to tell me that she was about to leave and had left dinner on the table.

"Don't you also live here?"

"Yes, I do. I am just going to work."

"Oh, you work during the night?" I asked.

Ligaya stretched her lips apart to form something that looked like a smile. "It actually depends on clients' wishes. I work during the day from home sometimes but I prefer working nights out."

"But Ligaya."

"Yes please."

"Where is Sebastian Baumann? He is the one I came to meet."

Ligaya rubbed her hands as if there was excessive hand cream she wanted to properly spread, looked at the ceiling, and said, "Mr. Baumann is out of Europe for the moment, but he is coming back soon. You will meet him, don't worry."

"Okay. By the way, how do you people survive this cold?" I only have two pairs of jeans and my jacket doesn't feel warm enough."

Ligaya stood up, holding the door as if ready to leave. "Tomorrow we can go shopping for a pullover and other things you may need."

That was the best thing I had heard so far. We were going shopping and I would get a chance to see the city. My only worry was that I didn't have the money to pay for those things.

"But I didn't bring money," I said, blushing with embarrassment.

"It's okay, I shall pay for everything and Sebastian will reimburse me when he comes," she said, lifting up her right hand to show me that money was not a big deal.

I got the feeling that Ligaya was being very nice to me, but she was simply being professional.

I was still not satisfied with Ligaya's details about Mr. Baumann, so I asked Ligaya the question that was still bothering me.

"Is this Sebastian's sleeping room? It looks quite empty." I didn't know where I got the courage to ask that.

Ligaya's facial expression was blank. I couldn't tell if she was hiding something or simply had no time to answer. "Uhmm... I better go to work before I miss my bus. See you later."

That night I enjoyed a warm bath for almost an hour. I filled the bathtub with water and laid in it luxuriously as I had seen people do in the movies. I thought of my sister, and I wished I had a phone to ask her how life was treating her in Dubai. If mother was still alive, she would be very proud of us, I thought. Sadness rose up in my throat. Fantasizing about my new life was the best way to stay positive. I got out of the bathtub, wrapped myself in a white towel and walked around the house that would become my new home. It was strange to realize that most of the rooms were locked. But I already had enough space to introduce myself to the European luxury I dreamed of.

Dinner was a small bowl of vegetable soup, a few pieces of a white slimy sausage and one slice of bread. I opened the fridge to check if there was something else to eat but I couldn't understand what was written on the packages. Everything was written in German, a language that I had never used before. I wondered if Ligaya found me fat and wanted to start putting me on a weight loss diet. Without any other option, I ate what she had left. I was very tired from the travel, so I went to sleep to prepare for exploring the city the next day.

In bed, all alone in the house, my mind started to wander. There was no Sebastian, no Sonia and no Ligaya— who had at least made me feel welcomed. What was I doing there? I woke up and decided to explore the house to see if I could find anything to give me some of the answers I was desperately searching for. First room, locked. Second room, locked. Running out of options, I took a break to try on a few shoes from the shelf in the corridor. Despite my worries, I pictured myself becoming "diaspora" in high heels and fake European hair. I thought of Aunty Rose and how she would say in admiration that the house looked like heaven, all white with spotless big glass windows. I returned to bed and slept soundly.

6

The next day Ligaya came home around noon and took me shopping. There was no driver this time. The man, who had picked me from the airport with Sonia, was apparently not Sebastian's driver.

Ligaya gave me a piece of paper with the address: Kleinestrasse 5, Blankenese.

"This is your address," she said, handing me the paper.

"Which address?" I turned to her.

"Here, this house. Everyone in Germany has a house number and a street name. It's very important to keep it with you or memorize it."

Memorizing had never been an issue for me, so from that day I knew where I lived.

Ligaya had called a taxi and it was already waiting for us in front of the gate. We were dropped off in front of a huge building with *Europa Passage* written in gold letters. We entered and Ligaya explained to me that it was easier to shop at malls because she can find everything in one place. She said this as if the alternative was walking on muddy streets searching for shops, as if the roads here were not clean asphalt and didn't have sides designated for pedestrians. We went straight to Zara and Ligaya picked out a few pullovers.

"Mutoni, go try on these ones. The color would suit you!" she said.

The color! Never have I ever bought clothes based on the color or material. They just had to fit me and be affordable. All I wanted was something big, fluffy and warm.

"But they are very thin," I answered, examining the pullovers.

"Those are made with wool and cashmere, a very warm material," she said.

"What is that? I just need something warm. Leave the wool or wolf thingy."

Ligaya laughed at me and began to explain.

"Touch this," she ordered. I touched the pullover.

"And touch this one," she grabbed another pullover from a different hanger. I touched it.

"Do you feel the difference?" No, I didn't. But I nodded my head, hoping she would not ask me to explain the difference. She continued, showing me that the tag for the first pullover had 20% wool while the other had 80% wool. She decided that we should buy the one with 80% wool because it's warmer. I was fine with it. After all, she was the one paying, so I accepted the expensive one.

Ligaya offered to show me a bit of the city. The weather was not very bad, so we walked slowly to the lake called Alster. Pedestrians and cars passed by, parents pushed their babies in strollers, and tourists took photos with selfie sticks. In the lake, ducks and swans were swimming. I stopped. Ligaya realized how I was staring, transfixed by the water and said, "This water used to calm me down 10 years ago when I arrived in this country. I still love to come here and just walk around."

Only half listening, I turned to her: "Ligaya, are those real ducks?"

"Yes."

"No, I mean real, like real living ducks not just for tourism."

She shook her head in surprise, "Of course they are a tourist attraction but they are also real."

"To whom do they belong then?" I asked in a voice close to whispering.

"To us. To everyone who lives in this city. To nature."

"Who eats them?"

Ligaya laughed so hard that tears rolled down her cheeks and she lowered to her knees.

What was funny about asking who eats the free meat since it belonged to everyone? Isn't it easier than running after animals in the forest hunting them down? Though that is done for pleasure, as a hobby, not because hunters are hungry or craving for meat. In fact, there is a license for that. Like a license for driving a car. Right? There was so much about this world I had yet to learn.

Still laughing, she asked, "Why would anybody eat them?"

"Because they are edible. This is meat Ligaya," I said, my confusion still apparent on my face.

She laughed even harder.

"Do you know how much a kilo of meat costs here?"

"No."

"First of all, it's illegal to kill these ducks. Second, meat in supermarkets is cheaper than someone running after ducks with a knife or a gun."

"Really?"

"Meat is cheaper than vegetables here. I mean, good organic vegetables. You'll realize that yourself soon."

My eyes opened wide. "I can't wait. I'll eat and gain weight and when I go home to visit, they will call me *Kibonge*. They will see money flowing." I brushed the left palm with the right one, showing how the money will flow.

"What? Wait," she exclaimed, "So you want to fatten yourself? Is that a good thing in Africa?"

"I don't know about all of Africa, but in Rwanda, yes. If you are skinny, it's seen as if you are poor or hungry. Most men, once their bank account starts growing, oh I am telling you, they grow a beer belly."

"And what about women?"

"We grow boobs and bums." We both laughed.

"Oh dear, here things are different. She pointed at a man crossing the road. "You see that guy? That fat one struggling to lift up his legs. He is among the poor people here, I can tell."

"Why?"

"The poor Germans, you know," she came closer and lowered her voice, "They are fat. They are the ones who eat too much meat and buy prepared food, spend most of their time watching TV, drink beer and live in tall buildings, which of course, have elevators to take everyone to their apartment so they won't burn calories on the stairs."

We ate bread and cheese that Ligaya had brought in her handbag and walked a few meters in silence. She glanced at her watch.

"We have to go. I have an appointment in two hours," she said.

There was no taxi driver so we took the bus and a boat to reach Sebastian's house with public transport.

While we stood at the bus shelter waiting for the bus that Ligaya said would come in three minutes, a group of teenagers passed by and shouted something in German to us. Something that I could tell wasn't like one of those compliments that young boys gave pretty women. Ligaya shouted an answer to them and they responded. Enraged, she showed them her middle finger while complaining to herself in her mother tongue.

"These people, they sometimes think that immigrants are their trash bins where they can throw all of their garbage." She said.

"What's wrong?"

The bus stopped and we entered.

"You won't believe what those boys said to us. They shouted: "*Ausslaender raus*. Foreigners and immigrants out.""

Shocked, I asked, "Why did they say that? We did nothing... We were just standing.""

"It's not their fault; they are just children who have no bad intention. They must have learned such words from their parents, or grandparents, or great grandparents. I don't know. Whatever. To live in this country, my dear, you need to grow a snakeskin and be ready to metamorphose according to each situation."

7

On Friday, Ligaya seemed to be avoiding me. Or maybe she was busy. Our conversation was limited to good morning, good night or 'I am leaving.' I spent my time watching movies on a huge TV screen that hung on the wall in the corner between the sofa and the piano and looking at pictures in fashion magazines. I used the free time to learn how to use a dishwasher and a microwave. Outside looked so gray and dark that I didn't wanted to leave the house.

I had just finished showering and was looking for something to wear when I heard a knock on the door. A young man in his mid-thirties who looked like a model from a Dior ad entered. He had long hair held back in a ponytail. He was wearing blue denim jeans and a white long sleeve t-shirt. He gave the impression of being very confident and comfortable in his body. In that moment, the blood flow increased in my whole body at the same time. I couldn't tell if his presence gave me arousal or fear. Likely, it was a mixture of both.

He extended his hand to me and I extended mine in return.

"Hi, I am Sebastian. Do you remember me? We spoke on Skype?" He asked, while looking deeply into my eyes with a smile that didn't show any teeth.

"Oh yes, I remember you. I am Mutoni." I sat on the bed straight, putting my box braids in order.

Sebastian grabbed the chair that was next to the bed and pulled it closer to me.

"How was your day? Sonia told me that you work a lot," I asked.

"Everyone in Germany works hard. I hope Sonia already explained everything to you."

"Like what? We didn't really talk much."

He sat up straight, "No problem. I will explain to you the basics. Where is your passport first?"

I reached for my passport from the back pocket of my suitcase and handed it over. If he had asked me for my heart from my body, I would have tried my best to offer it. I was ready to give him everything.

"Is it okay if I just call you Toni?"

"You talk like you already know me. That's actually what people back home call me."

"Okay, so let's get straight to business, Toni. Tell me about your experience."

Was he joking? "Experience in what?" I asked him, surprised.

His face became as cold as the weather outside.

"So, what did you and Sonia talk about the whole time? What did you think you had come here to do?"

"To meet you. You asked Sonia for a girlfriend, so she connected us," I replied, not understanding what he was implying.

He stood up, visibly upset, and pushed the chair away: "I asked for what? *Unglaublich.*"

My heart was beating quickly. I didn't know if I had said something wrong or if he was going to hit me.

He approached me and bent over, close enough that our foreheads almost touched. In a low but strong voice he said: "You look like you have no idea about your friend. Well, let me explain to you."

He sat on the bed next to me and grabbed my shoulders, forcing me look straight at him.

"Do you think I am too ugly to find a woman who would fall in love with me all of Hamburg? Or in all of Germany?" He asked me while spreading his arms as if painting the map of all 16 federal states that form the Federal Republic of Germany.

"No," I answered, my eyes blinking as fast as they could.

"Are you Sonia's best friend, as she told me?"

"No. We know each other from school and we grew up in the same neighborhood. But we are not..." He cut me short.

"Fine. Look, I spent so much money on you so that you could come here to replace Sonia. My clients were not happy with her anymore."

That made me more confused.

"Sebastian, to be honest I don't know what you are talking about. Sonia never told me about her work or mentioned anything like replacing her," I said, finally finding the right words.

"That is what they all say." He mocked me with laughter and then added, "I have been in this business for a long time. All the girls we bring here start by playing innocent, saying how they don't know why we brought them here. Then they cry and beg for their passports back and ask to fly back home immediately. In the end they always do the work. Some manage to pay off their debt and become free persons."

"But which work? I have a bachelor's degree in finance management, but of course I would do any available job since I am already here," I replied.

Visibly angered, he hit the frame of the bed.

"Enough theater, stop acting!" He stood up and added: "What about a degree in dick sucking or ass shaking?"

The face that had attracted me turned into a beast that I didn't want to look at. He moved to sit back down and in a calm voice said: "Listen, I met Sonia two years ago in Dubai where she worked at a hotel to give pleasure but was paid very low wages. I ordered her to my room and we discussed ahow she could come to work for me here. Of course, I arranged everything she needed like her visa and travel costs. The same as I did for you, right?"

"Yes," I agreed, and nodded my head.

He continued, "Sonia had to work for me in order to pay back everything I spent on her. Slowly my clients started complaining about her unpleasant performance. Luckily, one of my clients offered to pay off her debt and hire her in his nightclub on Repeerbahn Street. In order for me to accept, Sonia had to find a replacement. And that is you," he aggressively pointed a finger at my chest.

Prostitution. I had heard neighbors saying that Sonia was a prostitute abroad. Aunty Rose said it as well, but my desire to move abroad was burning so strong that I never thought twice about Sonia's offer. If I had thought about it, would I have said no? What alternatives did I really have for a future? I was coming to be an *indaya* or *malaya* in Germany, as mother used to call prostitutes. Why did Sonia choose me? There I was, in Europe. *Iburayi*. Helpless, with no chance to return home.

As panic set in, I lowered to my knees, begging him, "Please, I swear on my one and only sister's life that I didn't know what Sonia brought me here for."

Sebastian watched my emotional breakdown in silence.

My swollen eyes filled with tears and mucus began running from my nose. He made a disgusted face and stood up to leave. He walked to the door and back, and then he said, "You are lucky that I am a kind guy, so I will make things easier for you."

"Yes please, thank you so much Mr. Sebastian. Thank you," I almost kissed his feet to show how thankful I was.

"This is the limit of my kindness," he paused and walked back to me. "I will keep your passport and as soon as you finish paying off my debt you will be free to go. Is that clear?"

It didn't have to be clear, it just had to mention setting me free.

"Now stand up," he ordered.

Quickly I stood up, feeling relieved, and asked, "How long is that going to take? How much do I owe you?"

He raised his eyebrows and clapped his hands as if killing a mosquito. "Puuf, well, if you perform well then you will get many clients and you will finish quickly. Maybe one year. Maybe ten years. I don't know."

He left the room and closed the door behind him.

Immediately, Ligaya came into my room. She brought me a few pairs of transparent short dresses with matching G-string underpants, a box of makeup I had never seen before and some jewelry. She laid everything on my bed.

"That's all you will need for working from home," she said. "By the way, when you are getting ready for work, don't always put on makeup. Some clients like a clean face."

She left and I slapped my face, hoping that it was just a nightmare.

But everything was real.

8

A month passed without seeing any of the things I had expected in Germany. All I did was open my legs, close them, cry and repeat.

In movies I have watched, the bad European guys were the ones who wore ripped jeans, had a body full of tattoos and piercings, smoked a lot and spoke with vulgar language. My experience was far different from that. Sebastian's clients didn't fit those stereotypes. They were the kind of men who forced themselves to only talk about business, sports and politics while their brains rotate around what is hidden under women's clothes. They were the same as any other man who, after their wife gives birth and her body changes, search for what they feel is missing at home. Most of them had children and wives, to whom they had to lie that they were working overtime, watching soccer games with the guys or having business dinners with colleagues. The men were fat, skinny, old, gentle, and aggressive. Every type of man had passed between my legs for their pleasure.

Caring about what they said wouldn't have made my life any better, so I learned to simply answer "thanks" to both their compliments and insults. Ligaya had warned me to always show those men that I enjoyed the act. I had to pretend that I didn't feel like throwing up on them while they moaned and groaned on me without any affection.

The worst clients were the ones who thought they understood a woman's body better than a woman herself. Others considered themselves open minded because of their sexual adventures with different nationalities.

I will never forget Johannes, one of my first clients. He was 35 years old and had just returned from his mission in South Sudan. "You are very exotic, you know, and that is something I miss every time I come back home." That's how he opened up the conversation as we laid in bed. Of course, he expected me to reply "thanks", which I did with a fake smile.

Johannes picked up his trousers from the floor where he had dropped them while rushing to get inside me. He wore them and laid next to me with a bare chest.

"Why are you crying?" he asked me.

I wanted to cuss at him; instead I said, "Nothing, I am just tired."

He lifted my face from the pillow so that I could look at him and said, "Look, I don't believe your answer, but I would be happy to help you if I can."

"No thanks. Everything is fine," I replied.

He called himself a "humanitarian" but he was not ashamed of talking about how he learned a lot of sexual stuff from the young Sudanese girls in the refugee camp where he worked. His stories disgusted me. He talked about how women in Burundi always gave themselves easily to him for simply being white. If he was smart enough, he would have known that they wanted his money, not his skin color.

"You know what makes me stay in Africa?" He asked me.

I didn't know, and I wasn't interested in knowing, but since a short conversation was part of the service he paid for, I asked, "No, what is it?"

He said with a smile, "You guys make me feel special."

"What do you mean?"

"In Europe I am like a drop of water in the sea. Nobody knows me and nobody cares about me. I don't even get noticed by women that I'd consider unattractive."

"And in Africa?" I rolled my eyes at him.

"In Africa, oh… Africans. I don't understand why you guys come here," he said while putting on his t-shirt.

"The same reason you guys keep going to Africa. For a better life."

With an arrogant look he said, "Come on, don't be stupid." He walked a few steps away as if he was thinking about what to say and then he moved closer to my face.

"I don't mean to insult you, but look, here you are treated like shit. Right?"

I nodded my head and he continued, "In Africa I am respected everywhere. I mean everywhere. Beautiful women fight for me, I hang out with the elites and I am never seen as broke. *Muzungu* always have money," he faked laughter.

That truth hurt but he was right. Wasn't he?

Johannes had come home for holidays and when he heard from Sebastian that I was from Rwanda he wanted to practice *Kunyaza*, something he had seen in a documentary film about the sexual secrets of Rwandans.

On lucky nights when I didn't have a client, I cried myself to sleep. No single day passed without thinking of my sister. I didn't have a telephone or any other way to communicate with her. I was sure that she thought I had forgotten her and that I was living the best life traveling through Europe. These thoughts triggered the heavy thing that felt like an anaconda hanging around my neck— something that tightened as I thought of my life back home before my mother's death and only grew heavier as I remembered how I didn't say goodbye to my sister.

9

Ligaya was a 45-year-old professional escort from the Philippines. She met Sebastian there and had asked him to bring her to Germany. They made an agreement of how she would work for him and later start working independently while training his newcomers. She talked about how sex tourism was one of the biggest tourist attractions in her country.

That evening while we talked about the girls who worked for Sebastian before me, I asked Ligaya, "You said that some of those girls died in this country. Does Sebastian kill them or what?"

"My dear, don't abuse our friendship by asking too much. Sebastian is just the face you see but there are many people involved in this business."

Normally Ligaya did all of the house chores alone and I helped a bit when she asked me. That evening we folded the laundry together.

"Mutoni," she called me in a voice that was close to whispering.

"Yes," I replied.

"I think you should leave. This life here is not for you."

I wasn't sure if she meant it or if she was on a mission to find out for Sebastian if I was planning to escape.

"Why would you tell me that?" I asked her.

"Toni. I have been in this house for many years and the girls who have worked here successfully are different from you. You are not good for this business; you cry too much and I can see on your face that you are desperate."

"Humm," I breathed in deeply and exhaled.

"Keeping your passport is just a way of threatening you. Do you know how many people live in this country without papers?"

"No," I shook my head.

"Ask Nigerians," she said.

A long awkward silence passed between us.

She handed me the folded socks and underwear to arrange in the basket.

"But Ligaya, I don't know where to go and I don't have any money," I started to cry.

"Look, if anybody finds out that I told you anything, this will be the end of my life. But I don't want yours to end here. You are still young. Is this the life you want?"

I shook my head.

"So? You have to forget about what others have done to you, think of what you are doing to yourself."

I pulled a tissue from the pocket of my jeans and cleaned my nose.

"Stop crying. Tears won't get you anywhere in this life," she said, visibly upset.

"But I don't know where to go, Ligaya."

"How can you find where to go while you are still stuck here? In order to find your destination, you have to start the journey." She put her hand on my shoulders and lowered her voice. "You know, before I met Sebastian in Manila I used to work for another woman as an escort and she sent me to meet her clients in hotels or private houses. I never received any money from the clients because they paid her directly and she would give me 20% of their payment. Can you imagine 20% when I was the one doing the hard work?"

I nodded.

She shifted from her seat.

"And what did that bitch do? Nothing. I mean nothing except refusing to pay the money she owed me. She was getting rich from running the sex tourism business while I struggled to send my children to school and their father didn't help me at all. One day I decided that I wanted to become a professional escort and make my own money. When I told my boss about it, of course, she didn't like it. However, I needed to do it for my children and myself. I saw Sebastian and other men in the VIP bar of the hotel, and I went straight to them. I started a chat and asked if any of them would like my company to which they replied with a polite 'no thanks.' As if that could help me feed my family."

"Didn't you feel ashamed?"

"Ashamed of what?" She asked mockingly. "There is a level of life where shame means nothing. When you are on that level, shame exists only when you create it in your mind."

I nodded.

"So, I got a piece of paper from the hotel receptionist and wrote my phone number. I walked back to the table of Sebastian and his friends and I laid the paper in the middle of the table. I told them that if they change their minds, I will be at their service. Later that night, Sebastian called me to discuss this opportunity."

"And that's how you came here?"

"Yes. He didn't touch me at all. I have heard stories on Reeperbahn that he sleeps with men and just does this for business. Even the most beautiful of his girls, he doesn't touch them."

"But what if...."

"Shhhh," she glanced in the corridor.

The front door to the house opened.

"Hello!" Ligaya yelled.

I picked up the folded clothes to bring them in my room, and I heard footsteps coming from the corridor.

"Hey, Mutoni," Ligaya whispered. "That's Sebastian. Don't mention anything I told you. Okay?"

Sebastian stood waiting for me at the door of my room. I was startled by his presence, and as I turned to walk away he ordered me to stop.

"I am sorry, it's just that…"

"This is for you." He handed me a box of chocolates.

"Why?"

"My clients are happy with your services. Congratulations on completing your first month."

Disgust grew heavy in my throat and I wished I were strong enough to smash him against the wall. Instead, I gathered enough saliva in my mouth and spat in his face.

In less than a second, he dragged me to the floor by my hair as my hands scrambled to prevent him from pulling it out. "Sebastian," I screamed his name.

Imposing like a giant, Sebastian stood over me and I could tell what was coming. It wasn't the first time. He slid his belt off and immediately recognized the clank of the buckle as he wrapped it around his hand. The all too familiar sounds sent flames of fear all over my body.

Flooded with agonizing sensations, I coiled my body into a fetal position in an attempt to protect my head.

Nightfall was coming and the winter remained harsh outside. I cried for help, but there was nobody else in the house except Ligaya.

Whack! The first hit. Powerful, hot pain seared from my back.

Whack! This time it struck my shoulders. I cried.

I begged him to stop but instead he only kept beating me harder.

I choked my scream— Hearing it only made him angrier.

It was only when he heard me gasp for air that he called "Ligaya."

"Yes sir," she answered from the kitchen.

"Clean up this mess," he said coldly, as if he wanted her to sweep the floor.

He kicked me one final time and said, "Make sure you drink enough water."

Then he left.

10

When pain becomes extreme, the body has its own superpower ability to neutralize it. From that day, I could tell that Sebastian lived in a world where violence was the norm. He had punished me violently whenever I disobeyed his clients, but this time, I couldn't take it anymore.

I stayed in bed feeling like my ribs were cracking; pain radiated from every area of my body. Sebastian didn't come to talk to me but I could hear him in the house chatting and smoking with people. Ligaya entered my room only to ask if I wanted to eat or to join her for a short walk in the park. It became clear to me that I would die in that house. I decided that I would at least die trying to rescue myself.

A few days later, when Ligaya went to meet a client at the hotel I asked if we could go together but she refused. Shortly after, Sebastian also left the house. "I need to get a few things from the supermarket," he told me while putting on his shoes. I heard his car starting and driving away.

When I walked to get water from the kitchen and passed Sebastian's office, the room that he normally kept locked, I realized that it was open. Ligaya had told me that it was where he kept important documents. I pushed the door, walked inside and looked around at the files and papers arranged properly on the shelf. To my surprise, my passport was laying on the table. With my hands shaking, I picked it up and ran back to my room. I pushed the passport under the bed; no, there the cleaning lady would find it. I moved it to my drawer; no, here Ligaya would see it. But the pocket of my jacket, too, was very dangerous in case Sebastian found it. After a moment of running around searching for the safest place to hide it, I finally pushed it under my pillow. I was the only one who slept in that bed, except for the men who spent some nights on it. However, they had no interest in checking under the pillow, they had other priorities.

On the third day, I was still recovering from the pain, but I had a visitor.

My visitor was a man who looked about 60 years old. I couldn't guess his age well. Excessive consumption of alcohol, no doubt, made him look much older than he was. He said nothing except a formal "Hallo, my name is Moeller. Mister Moeller." He had already paid and was in a hurry to get it done. His oversized body made me panic. I had enough pain already and I couldn't stand his weight on top of my wounds. As he started touching me, sliding his hands around my waist and grabbing my butt, I made sure to keep my hands on his manhood. He released himself from me and took off his winter coat. He hung it on the door of my wardrobe and unzipped his trousers. His trousers fell to the floor and I could tell the size of his penis through his tight underwear. I grabbed him again pressing hard and moving my hands up and down very fast. His body started shivering and he pressed himself against my half naked thighs to feel the warmth of my body. He let out a moan and collapsed on the floor.

Mister Moeller wasn't moving and it didn't look like normal resting. He was still breathing. I touched his chest and could feel that his heart was still beating.

Sebastian was in the living room having drinks with other men. I could hear them laughing loudly. I tried to imagine how many of them would come to take turns on me after the alcohol kicked in. I pulled out 50 Euros from the wallet that had fell out of his trousers. I knew that if Sebastian caught me it would mean death, but I was dying slowly anyway. What did I have left?

"It's now or never," I whispered to myself as I locked the door. The window I had opened to get fresh air was my opportunity to leave. I grabbed my passport from under the pillow where I had hid it, took the 50 stolen Euros and pulled on my clothes. I couldn't find any shoes, however, because we always left them in the corridor. What would I say if Sebastian saw me wearing shoes? I didn't want to risk losing the only chance I had.

Like many other houses in Blankenese, Sebastian's house didn't have a huge fence surrounding it; instead, it was enclosed by a short green fence. It wasn't like back home where they would surround the houses with high brick fences lined on top with pieces of broken glasses to hurt thieves who dared to climb. As if that's not safe enough, they'd add an additional metal gate with wires on top.

I climbed through the window, jumped down into the street and ran. I ran so fast that even a bullet couldn't catch me. I ran on an icy road with nothing but socks covering my feet. I ran until I was out of breath. Finally, I stopped to check if anybody was following me. Seeing no one, I ran again until I reached a place where people were entering and exiting buses, the only place I could find shelter. I entered the next bus without knowing its destination and wrapped my coat around myself to hide my head.

The warmth took over my body and I fell asleep. A woman in a black winter coat and a grey scarf in the seat next to me shook me awake as she struggled to leave. "*Darf ich raus,*" she said, and I looked around. We were the only ones left in the bus. "Excuse me, what did you say?" I asked her.

"May I go out," she said with a smile.

I stood up to let her pass and followed her. "Where are we?" I asked.

"That's the central station of Hamburg," she said, pointing at the building opposite the street. "You know where you have to go?" She asked.

"Yes, thank you," I said.

"Please," she answered and walked away. This is a mistake that I would later learn is unique to Germans when they speak English.

11

The tall buildings that surrounded the area gave me nausea. They looked like they were falling down towards me in slow motion.

It was quickly turning into night and the initial thrill of escaping Sebastian's house turned into the horror of dying homeless on the street. Everything on my left looked like everything on my right and I didn't know where to start the journey. I remembered what Ligaya had told me: "Crying won't get you anywhere in this life." I closed my eyes for a moment, trying to turn off my worries.

I had been sitting for a long time in the bus shelter, and everybody was looking at me. Or maybe it was just all in my head. Pedestrians walked quickly in all directions. I wrapped myself in the oversized coat I had taken from my last client to keep warm, but I still shivered in the cold. In contrast, the warm air coming out of my mouth looked as if I was exhaling smoke.

I let out a groan of pain as I adjusted myself to a comfortable position which made the woman at the end of the bench look at me. That woman tightened her lips and stretched them to a forced smile. What if she was sent by Sebastian to search for me, I thought. I decided to leave. Ligaya had said that there are many people in Hamburg that are involved in Sebastian's business. I stood up and forced my legs to walk. I would walk somewhere. Anywhere. My legs shook with fear and coldness, while my stomach was in pain from hunger. I stumbled and fell back on the bench. Helplessly, I broke into tears. It was impossible to stick to the advice of Ligaya. Yes, tears wouldn't get me anywhere but where was I going anyways? For a second, I wished I could have stayed at Sebastian's house.

I shook my head while crying.

A woman approached me. She looked around 35 years old, or maybe older. I don't know. I realized that I haven't been close enough to white people to be able to accurately guess their age. The only ones I had interacted with were the tourists in Rwanda who bought colorful Kitenge in the market and took photos of food. Or the ones who considered Nyamirambo the coolest part of Kigali and would walk around taking photos of the street DJs, the colorful small houses, the graffiti on the walls and the women carrying their babies on their back as if they were in a museum. Or maybe in a zoo.. All I ever spoke to them was "Hi *Muzungu*" or "Good morning *Muzungu*." Sometimes, I helped them to find a location that they couldn't find on Google Maps. They always responded with a smile. A smile that didn't clarify if they wanted to have a longer conversation or if they were irritated by their new nickname but were trying to behave politely.

"A*lles gut?*" She asked.

"Yes," I nodded, trying to discreetly wipe off my tears.

The woman handed me a tissue to wipe my nose and moved next to me. Close enough for our shoulders to almost touch. Close enough that I wished she could take me in her arms and whisper, "Everything will be fine." But she didn't. That woman was raised to respect people's privacy to the point where she could never offer a stranger a hug.

"Are you fine?" The woman asked again. This time in English.

"I want to die," I cried.

"Oh dear no. Why?"

The tenderness in her voice gave me relief. I crunched my teeth together, wiped my nose, glanced at the woman and looked down.

"I am Anna. What's your name?" She asked while offering to shake my hand.

"Mutoni."

"Is that name Ugandan or Rwandan?" Anna asked, and an alarm went off in my head, alerting me that Anna may be working with Sebastian.

"Who are you?" I turned to her.

Anna looked at me in surprise, "What do you mean? Anna. I just told you my name."

"Yes. Who are you? What do you know about Rwanda? Whom do you work for?"

"Well, I visited Rwanda two years ago," Anna started to talk and then paused. She glanced at her watch and then continued, "While working for a German NGO in Uganda, but I visited Kigali a few times with my ex-boyfriend. I loved how clean and very organized the city is, compared to Kamplala where I was living."

"Look, if Sebastian sent you to bring me back, tell him that I would rather die on this street instead of going back to that house of torture. You guys are criminals." I let out a scream followed by crying. "Criminals. God will burn you all in hell," I yelled at Anna.

Anna held her arms open. "May I hug you?" I nodded.

"What's going on Mutoni? I am sorry if I said something wrong," Anna whispered softly. I tried to talk but I couldn't. I cried. I cried all the tears I had kept inside for so long. The tears I didn't let out when all the men satisfied their fantasies on me in Blankenese and the tears that were never released after my mother's death.

"My bus will come in two minutes. How can I help you before I go?" Anna asked as she ushered me slowly to sit up straight.

"Please don't leave me alone. I have nowhere to go..." I stretched the last syllable with a sound that was somewhere between a sigh and a groan. "They will kill me. I know they will."

"Who will kill you?" Anna looked at me in confusion.

While sobbing, I removed my coat and pulled down my shirt, exposing my shoulders and my snake-skinned body. Anna saw the marks of Sebastian's belt on my shoulders and looked away.

"Who did this to you?" Tears filled her eyes.

"Mutoni. Who did that to you?" Anna repeated.

"The man who brought me here. He had men who raped me, and whenever I disrespected his clients, he would beat me. I ran away from his house and I don't know where to go. Please help me. I beg you."

"Who is that asshole?" Anna was enraged.

Hunger, coldness and tiredness had consumed all my energy. My mind went blank before I could answer, and I began to see my mother's sad face staring at me with disappointment. I laid down flat on the bench.

I burst out crying and Anna patted my back.

"*Alles gut,*" she whispered. "It's fine Mutoni. It will all be fine." She soothed me.

At this point, my whole body was numb.

The bus stopped in front of us. People got out and others got in.

Anna stood still, watching the bus drive away.

She turned to me. "Come, let's go eat something. You must be hungry."

"I can't move anymore. My body cannot," I answered.

Anna ran to the other side of the road and entered a big building. A few minutes later, she returned with brownish bread that looked like a snake twisting itself to form multiple circles. She handed it over to me. "Eat this pretzel. It will help you get some energy."

"Thanks," I said while stuffing the bread in my mouth.

"And this is peppermint tea to warm up your body," she handed me a paper cup with a plastic lid on it. I took a sip. It was hot water with some flavor; something that

I was sure nobody in Rwanda would call tea. It was maybe a type of hot water one would drink if they were sick. Its taste was close to *Umwenya*, some herbs that my mother used to force me to drink when I had a cold, and I was comforted by the idea of home.

"Look, I can't take you with me. Maybe I will help you to find a women's shelter nearby. You can sleep there, and they will help you with whatever you need," Anna said.

"Please imagine if you were in my situation. How would people treat you if you were lost in Rwanda?" I went on my knees begging.

"Okay, okay. It's okay Mutoni. Stop kneeling," she paused for a moment, then added, "Let's go." She held me by the shoulders and pulled me up.

I was not sure if Anna decided to help me out of kindness or if she felt embarrassed because of all of the people staring at us.

"Thank you very much Anna."

We entered Hauptbahnhof, the Hamburg train station, and stopped by the big screen that was hung close to the ceiling. It looked like what I had seen in the airport.

"The Ubahn is leaving in five minutes. Let's walk to the platform."

"What is that?"

"It's the type of tram we have to take to my place. You see that red sign of U2?" She pointed to the screen and I nodded.

"We will take the one going to Schlump."

"Is that where you live?"

"No. From Schlump we can walk to my place or take the bus. I live in Altona."

"Thanks a lot. May god bless you." I hugged her.

"I don't believe in God, but thanks. Come, let's run." She pulled my hand.

We walked through crowds of people running in all directions. In the middle of that chaos, some people were pulling suitcases while others pushed babies in strollers. I wondered where all those people were coming from, or where they were going.

To reach the train we had to take escalators. As we approached them, I held Anna's hand secretly wishing I had time to practice stepping on them as I had done at the airport when I left Rwanda. My first time seeing escalators was at Kanombe airport, but there I had enough time; I had stood in front of them, watching how they move up, and I had observed how other passengers came and stepped on them with an ease that made me feel ashamed. Later during my journey, I had to struggle with using them again during my layover in Brussels. When I finally arrived in Germany, I wished to never see them again.

"What's wrong?" Anna asked, my hands gripping hers tightly.

"I can't walk on these kinds of stairs," I answered her.

"But you don't need to walk, you just stand on them and they will bring you up. Come on."

"No, please." My answer came too late. Anna had already pulled me to stand behind her onto the moving stairs. When we stepped off the escalator, I was relieved. Anna started laughing.

Anna was 30 years old but when she laughed she looked ten years younger.

Her long winter manteaux made her upper body look shorter than her lower body.

She wore cropped jeans that were tight around her waist and loose everywhere else. As if her trousers were not short enough, she folded them up to show off her colorful, striped woolen socks. To me, those socks looked too thick to be worn in sneakers. But what did I know about German fashion?

"I am sorry to laugh at you," she said, suppressing a giggle. "I never thought that escalators could be such a struggle."

The tram took about 20 minutes. I told Anna my journey starting with my mother's death: The event that separated me from my sister, gave me depression and triggered my departure from Rwanda for a man whom I knew nothing about. Anna listened with empathy and when she took the keys out of her coat to open the door, I stopped to check my surroundings.

"Are we already at your home?" I asked in surprise. I hadn't realized that we had left the train and already walked for about 20 minutes.

"Yes. We will take the stairs. I live up on the third floor."

I continued talking as we walked upstairs. Anna squeezed my hands as I talked about the month that I had spent in Sebastian's house. She listened and tears ran down her cheeks as if she was watching everything happening in real time.

"You don't have to say it all," Anna said while sobbing.

"It's okay. I am happy to just let it out for the first time."

I continued, describing how men of all characters and sizes took rounds of pleasure on me. I told her everything until the day I decided to escape.

Anna hugged me tightly. It was a hug that meant "I am here for you." And a hug that meant "What you have been through shouldn't happen to any human."

Anna's apartment was so small that I felt sorry for her whole family which squeezed into the tiny space. She had a sleeping room with one small bed and a shelf, a kitchen, a living area with a small sofa and a bathroom. I wondered where Anna's visitors slept, where she stored her food and where she hung her laundry to dry.

"Get a drink from the fridge or grab something to eat," Anna gestured to the fridge that was next to the sofa in the corner. "Feel at home."

When I opened the fridge, there was nothing I could eat in that moment. One cold cucumber, four carrots, half of an avocado, and some other vegetables that I didn't recognize. There were a few other familiar items like cheese, tomato juice, Soja milk and tofu but I didn't touch them. I decided to wait for Anna who had rushed into her room to talk to her mother on telephone. I looked at the pictures in all the magazines in the box next to the sofa.

After a moment Anna reappeared with a bright smile and sat next to me.

"Saturday we will go home together," she said.

"Tomorrow? Which home?"

"To my parents' house. They live in Willheim ,a village in the south of Germany about eight hours from here by train. My mother just said you can stay with her there for a few days."

"Really? That is very kind of you, thanks."

"Do you really want to go back to Rwanda, or do you want to stay in Germany?" Anna asked, staring deep in my eyes as if to pull out the answer.

"I don't know," I paused. "I have nobody left back home but I also don't know anybody here and I don't understand your language. I think it would be best for me to return to Rwanda instead of roaming aimlessly in Europe."

She held my hands in hers and said, "Think about your decision. My mother has an idea of how we can help you live in Germany. Okay? We will discuss about it when we are in Gernsbach."

Anna stood up and brought a small white container from the fridge. She grabbed her kitchen chopping board which was so big that it looked like a dining table in itself, then called me to come help her prepare dinner.

"Let's set the table."

"For dinner? What time is it?" I asked.

Anna glanced at her watch and said, "Almost 10 PM. I will sit with you and drink tea because I don't eat anything after 7 PM." That was strange but I didn't say anything.

Dinner consisted of a dark bread covered with seeds and grains so large I was afraid that if I swallowed them they would leave scratches in my throat, an avocado the size of an egg, butter, different types of smelly cheese, round slices of cucumbers, one boiled egg and chopped carrots.

"Enjoy," Anna said as she plugged in the kettle to boil water for tea.

I looked at everything on the table and wondered which one was "dinner" because it didn't look like a meal to me. In Blankenese, Ligaya usually made soup for dinner. Back then, I was worried that I would wake up in the middle of the night to eat because soup before bed was like sleeping on an empty stomach, but slowly I adjusted.

"Is this all you eat for dinner?" I asked.

"Yes. We call it *abendbrot* in German. Normally it goes with sausages or ham, but I am vegetarian. Most people eat it between 6 and 7 PM."

"What is vegetarian?"

"I don't eat meat. I do that for my health and for the environment, you know."

No wonder why she looks hungry, I thought. No meat, tiny portions of food and she stopped eating at 7PM. I ate only the egg, pretending I wasn't hungry while Anna drank a glass of greenish warm water.

We cleaned up the table, put things back in the fridge and washed the dishes by hand. When we finished, Anna pulled out a box from under her bed and brought out a black sack that looked like a mattress cover and a white bed sheet. I had never used a sleeping bag before. I struggled to get inside of it and finally settled by covering myself with it like a normal blanket.

"Good night. Do you know where the toilet is, in case you wake up in the night?" Ana asked, wearing only a loose white t-shirt and underwear. It was cute how she thought I would get lost in a flat the size of my living room back home.

"Good night Anna. Thank you again," I answered. Unlike other Germans, Anna wasn't worried that I would steal her valuable things in the night.

Instead of sleeping that night, I cried. My heart felt heavy and I needed to ease the weight of the lump forming inside my throat. I cried thinking of how my mother used to tell me that she would fight for my happiness until her last breath, which she did, but now that she wasn't there anymore who was going to fight for me? I cried, wondering how Tendeza had probably tried to contact me from Dubai and couldn't reach me. Now that I was free, I decided I was finally going to fight for myself and others.

The next day Anna brought me a bag of clothes she wasn't wearing anymore. "Check if there is something you can wear from here," she said, handing me the bag.

"Anna!" I called.

"Yes?" She answered.

"Can I borrow your phone to use Facebook? Or maybe your computer? I want to check if my sister wrote me about her new life in Dubai."

"Sure," she brought her Macbook and opened Facebook.

I logged in and went straight to check my inbox but there was no message from Tendeza.

12

On the day my mother left us, she took a piece of me with her.

It was on a Friday afternoon in a 5-bed hospital ward. I leaned over to comb her hair and she grasped my hand. She wouldn't let it go. She struggled to tell me something but could not manage to finish it. Her stare became as cold as the metal bed she had laid on for two months. At this point, fear coursed through my veins as my heart thumped loudly.

"Mama," I whispered.

No answer.

"Mama," I screamed while shaking her.

I didn't care about being quiet for other patients.

The cold had taken over her body. Her hands were motionless and her face filled me with dread. The face that I loved very much, the same face that used to make me feel safe knowing that it will always be there for me.

"Maaama," I cried hopelessly while collapsing on top of her.

I knew that we needed a miracle, but there was none.

My mother was gone.

Comforting hands rested on my shoulder. I heard soft, soothing whispers in my ears. The words of nurses meant little to me as the life of the person who gave me mine ended. I apathetically watched nurses cover my mother and take her away. She had been fighting cancer and as her days of suffering came to an end, mine began. The neighbors gossiped about how she died of HIV. According to them, there was nothing else a single mother with two children from different fathers could have died from.

A few weeks later I sold my mother's restaurant, unable to keep it running while paying for the debts she had left behind. Nirere owed me ten thousand. Nirere took a bag of rice from my shop; I am sorry about your loss, but I really need the money. Nirere had borrowed 20 thousand from me when she couldn't pay your school fees. Nirere this, Nirere that. Some of those people had agreements they had signed with her, others showed me messages that they had written to each other and others had nothing at all but talked in a convincing way. I quickly gave up and just paid them all.

Tears ran down my face as I recalled this memory in the train from Hamburg where I sat by the window looking outside. I remembered everything like it was yesterday.

13

Willheim was calm.

The center of the city didn't have skyscrapers like the ones I had seen in Hamburg. Its train station didn't have pedestrians who filled the streets, rushing in all directions like disturbed ants. From the train station to the house, there were no bicycles with boxes attached on the back where children squeezed inside, tied with seatbelts like goats I have seen in the suburbs of Kigali.

Anna's parents lived in a big white house in front of the *Kurpark*. It was a park that I would later learn was only for tourism. Everything, except for walking on the designated path or sitting on the benches placed deliberately in each corner, was strictly prohibited. Apparently, there are playgrounds for things such as children playing or relaxing in the grass.

"Welcome. I am Sybille. Sybille Kranz," Anna's mother came close to hug me and a shaggy white-haired dog followed closely behind.

"Thank you. I am Mutoni Christine. My friends call me Toni."

"Anna! Oh you have not told me that she is very beautiful. Is this your real hair?" She said, sliding her hands through my box braids.

"Ah mama," Anna shrugged and lead the way into the living room after kissing her mother on each cheek.

Sybille kept her eyes on me while Anna told her the story of a crazy man that we had met in the Hamburg train station. While we changed from the tram that brought us from Anna's house to the ICE train taking us to Karlsruhe, a drunken man had shouted something and Anna shouted back to him. Later in the train, Anna had explained to me that the guy had asked if I had a valid visa, to which Anna had responded that he should worry about his alcohol consumption instead of my residency status.

Sybille stood up and brought a tray with cookies, a teapot, three cups and milk.

"Stupid people exist here. But you have not worry," she said, holding my shoulder with one arm. Her English wasn't perfect but I appreciated the fact that she made an effort to speak it. I could understand everything she meant.

"Where is Bernhard?" Anna asked.

"Oh *Schatz*," Sybille held her forehead, "I cannot anymore, he is in *Pflegeheim* but tomorrow we pick him." She continued to shake her head.

"Mutoni, make yourself comfortable and feel welcome. I need to talk with Sybille, and we will be back in a second," Anna said. She walked to the next room with her mother.

She calls her mother "Sybille," as if she is her friend or little sister, I thought. I ate all the cookies and drank a cup of milk, but I didn't touch the tea.

The furniture looked like it was 100 years old; the tables stood on thin legs and an unstable-looking sofa made me wonder how it carries the weight of all the people it was designed to support. There was a big painting covering half of the wall, photographs of Anna as a child alongisde a boy in a wheelchair and photographs of a woman who looked like a younger version of Sybille and a man with shoulder length hair. The carpet was as white as the snow I had seen in Hamburg.

Anna returned with her mother and they sat on each side of me.

"So, Mutoni," Anna said, nervously brushing her jeans with her hand as if removing some dust.

"Yes. Say it to her Anna," Sybille said and moved closer to me.

Fear grew inside me wondering what kind of news was about to come.

"Sybille said you could stay here. You can live here, with her."

My eyes opened and closed, and my mouth formed the biggest smile it had made since I left Rwanda. I hugged Sybille.

"Thank you very much." Tears of joy filled my eyes. Sybille had seen a vulnerable child in me who needed a family and she gave me one, I thought.

"But to do this would mean that you will help her around the house. You can see that she is becoming old so there is a lot of things she can't do anymore. Therefore, she would stop paying people who do it and you would help her. What do you think?

"Anna, I will clean, cook, and scrub the floors. And if she wants me to wash her I would also do it," I pulled Anna's hand, "I don't know how I can thank you enough."

"I will be your family. We have a way to help you," Sybille said.

"One more thing," Anna said, pointing at a photo of her and the boy in a wheelchair. "This is my older brother, Bernhard. He was born with a physical disability. Three times a week he goes to the nursing home but since you'll be here, there is no need to take him there anymore. Mama will show you how to care for him. Is that okay? We still have to talk to him though."

What was not okay? Taking care of her brother and helping around the house? It wasn't like they didn't have machines for almost everything; she made it sound so hard as if I would have to mop the floor with my tongue.

"Thank you, mama. I will do everything as you wish."

"Oh *bitte*, call me Sybille," she emphasized the last "e" to make sure I understood it well. She wasn't like one of those women who change their names to Mama Diane or Mama Fils as soon as they have their first born and later, as they grow old, turn it into "Tate, Bibi, Mukecuru." Those women get offended when you call them by their birth name; it means that you don't respect them. But each culture has its own complications and specialties, so I had to train myself to call a woman the age of my grandmother by her first name.

Sybille showed me the house, demonstrating how and where I will have to clean. We went downstairs and she showed me my sleeping room in the basement.

"There is also a shower and toilet for you in the next room," Sybille said.

"But here feels colder than upstairs. Can I sleep in one of the rooms upstairs?

"Really?" Anna said mockingly, "Be happy you have water and electricity here 24/7. Is that not a luxury? I remember my house in Uganda didn't…"

"Anna has lived in Africa, you know? So, we agreed this room is good for you," Sybille said. I nodded in acquiescence.

"Oh, and by the way, you will be cooking your own food as well," Anna said.

"Uhmm okay."

"I mean, I suppose you won't like the European cuisine. So, you better cook yourself potatoes or whatever else you like," Anna explained.

14

In one week, I was married.

We drove to Denmark, where we met other Europeans who wanted to marry foreigners under the conditions that their country wouldn't allow, and we were married.

In order to keep me in Germany legally, the Kranz family had been talking with a lawyer who suggested that the best way would be a marriage arrangement. Bernhard suggested that as long as the arrangement wouldn't affect their family properties, we could marry and divorce after I received citizenship. The lawyer confirmed that Bernhard's option was easier than taking me through the asylum process where they would have to invent stories like female mutilation, homosexuality, war and other atrocities that would not have made sense because I was from Rwanda. Besides, such topics have been overused, the lawyer had said. Through marriage, I would have a residence permit, which I could later use to apply for German nationality. We had to hurry the process before my three-month tourist visa expired.

Anna met us in Denmark with Stella, her colleague from Ghana, who she had arranged as my witness. Stella was a project manager at Plan International. She walked with confidence and elegance, laughed whole heartedly and spoke with an easiness that made me jealous of her. Her life was exactly how I imagined mine would look like in Europe. I wondered the reasons behind her migration, but couldn't dare to ask. When Anna realized how I kept my eyes on Stella, she told me that Stella was her supervisor. She was a Ghanaian expat who came to work in Germany. "She doesn't speak any German even though she has been living here for two years. It's a shame, isn't it?" Anna whispered while Stella chatted with Bernhard. I said nothing.

We made our vows and signed marriage documents clearly stating that I would have no rights to any family property and income. Afterwards, we had dinner in a fancy restaurant before driving back to Germany overnight. The lawyer would take care of the process of getting our marriage recognized in Germany and everything else.

A month later, I held my residence permit with 'Kranz, Mutoni Christine' written on it. My heart jumped to the highest level it had ever been before. "I am a German resident," I screamed with joy to Sybille who was observing my reaction, and ran to show it to Bernhard who was watching a documentary on his computer.

"I am Germaaaaan," I shouted.

"What?" He turned to see if I was fine and I showed him the residence permit. "Look!" I said. Bernhard examined the card, front and back, and said, "You are not German. You are allowed to live legally in Germany. Those are two different things." I lifted up the left corner of my upper lip and shrugged, "Whatever."

The fine details didn't matter in that moment, I was over the moon knowing that I could walk around without worrying about what could happen if the police stopped me; I would soon get medical insurance and go to the best doctors; I could travel in other European union countries; I could buy a sim card for the old iPhone Sybille had given me; and, finally I was able to borrow books from the community library.

Sybille, who was between 65 and 75 years old (I could not guess her age due to the foundation and concealer she always applied on her face as soon as she left her bed), treated me as a mother, and I made a promise to myself to please her.

Sybille hung my daily schedule on the wall in the kitchen where she had other important notices. The wall was clogged with tickets for jazz and classical concerts, three invitations to fundraising events to feed hungry children in Africa, an invitation to the community art exhibition that would raise funds to support poor women in Timor-Leste, a Friday appointment to Choco brown where she went once a month to get a tan when she would come back home with a pale-yellow brownish skin color and her appointment to the dentist. Next to that hung another paper with the telephone numbers of the police, ambulance and fire brigade.

"You see this telephone number," Sybille said after we finished breakfast one day. "That one of *Feuerwehr.*"

"Yes," I nodded.

"How is called in English?" She asked.

"What?"

"The people you call for example if the house has fire. Like burning," she slid her hand through her silky blonde hair.

"Ah, it's called the fire brigade," I said.

"Thanks. It's very important to keep it here in the kitchen. If fire is on, directly call them. Okay?"

"Yes, I will."

"You have that also in Africa? I can imagine too much fire there when people cook on wood."

In Africa!

"Well mama, uhm…mama Sybille, I have actually not traveled to all of Africa. I was born in Rwanda and I grew up there. The first time I left was to come here. But at home we didn't cook on wood. However, I could help you do research on the internet so you can find better information." The urge to explain to her that Africa, as a continent, is different from what she had watched on TV, was stronger than my patience but I had to remember my place in her house.

15

Many things at the house took me time to figure them out.

For example, separating the garbage. All plastics and metal had to go in a container with a yellow cover, except the bottles and cans which had to be returned to receive money back; papers and cartons went together in a container with a green cover; the leftovers from food went in a brown container, except things like fruits or vegetable peels which had to go in another container in the garden to become compost; glass bottles went in another black container; and whatever else was left, went in the grey container.

Whenever Sybille looked in one of the trash bins inside the house, she would complain that I had mixed it all up.

"Mutoni, what is this?" She called for me from the kitchen while I was scrubbing the toilets.

"Yes please," I ran to find her holding an empty tomato can in front of the trash bin that I thought was for everything.

"You don't make *Muelltrenung* in Africa?" She asked.

"What does that mean? Sorry mama Sybille, I don't understand well…" She cut me short.

"Don't mama me. Respect me by calling my name."

"Sorry Sybille," I apologized, looking down.

"So you mix all in Africa, or what? Plastic, paper, composts…everything together?" She was upset and throwing her hands left and right as if painting a picture of messy Africa full of garbage.

"We do. I mean, in Rwanda we do separate garbage. I don't know about other African countries. In fact, Sybille, my home city is cleaner than here." She gave me a skeptical look and walked to the living room.

My daily activities included taking the dog for a morning walk in the park, cleaning the house's three bathrooms, taking out the trash bins (yes, the German garbage also has space in the house), cleaning the whole house (four bedrooms, one living room, a storage, a kitchen, dining room, and office room), doing the laundry and taking Bernhard wherever he wanted to go.

16

Ironing was the task I hated most but listening to
music as I did it made it at least tolerable.

I would listen to the songs of Kamaliza, Mani
Martin, Bruce Melodie and Masamba. I didn't always
have the chance to keep the music on. Sometimes
Sybille would ask me to switch it off because it was too
loud, or she would tell me stories as I ironed.

"Hi *meine Liebe, ja...*" Sybille was talking to
someone on the phone as I ironed nearby. I was
listening to Ishiraniro of Phocas Fashaho, a song that
sounded like it was written for me. It was a song that
contained the advice I wished I could have been given
before leaving Rwanda.

"Toni. Mutoni!" She gestured to the loudspeaker
while I sang along with the chorus, too distracted to
hear her yells, *"Ntuzashukwe n'amatara yaka
imiturirwa itatse uruyange ngo ucyeke ko ari
paradizooo..."* I sang, swinging my head left and right.

"Toni, your music," Sybille said loudly and I switched it off.

"*Ist alles gut? Ja, kein problem*. Mutoni come talk to Anna."

I switched off the iron box and put it properly on the side.

"Yes, Anna. How are you?"

"I am good. There is something I can't help myself from sharing with you," Anna said.

"Tell me!"

"There is this guy Nicolas, a colleague of mine from Burundi, and he has lived here for 20 years. But guess what he just called me…"

"What?"

"Can you believe that he insulted me by calling me racist? Can you imagine that?" Anna sounded very upset.

"What happened?"

"Apparently, last night the police arrested him on his way home."

"Oh, no!"

"He lives in Wandsbek, a neighborhood of Hamburg that has many Black people. He said that he was walking to his house from the train station and a guy passed by him, running fast, and behind him he heard people shouting at him to stop. Confused, he just kept walking."

"Okay," I nodded.

"Then, all of a sudden, two policemen pushed him on the ground and handcuffed him. He started asking what was going on because he had done nothing, of course, while one of the policemen began asking questions."

"That happened on a normal road? But why did they arrest him?"

"Because, after they had taken him to their office and checked his residence, they called our boss as the guy had insisted. Then, they apologized that they have mistaken him for the other guy that they were chasing. So, why would he walk in a narrow street between houses in the night when he knows that he lives in a risky neighborhood? That's what I asked him and he started yelling at me, saying that the neighborhood is safe but I know, I have been there, it's a place where you see only immigrants and you never know what could happen."

"Okay, but now he is free?"

"Yeah, only because our boss had to drive there and get him out. So, when Nicolas called me racist because I said that the police were doing their job and there was no way they knew he wasn't the one they were chasing …you know, I said that he doesn't know me well. I told him that I have lived in Uganda for two years and my ex-boyfriend was Black, so I am not his image of a typical white German. I added that you, my sister-in-law are black, and I love you."

"What? You didn't have the right to argue with your colleague. His life here is totally different from yours in Uganda, and besides, you don't have a single idea…no idea at all about what he is going through," I screamed on the phone. Sybille rushed in to see what was going on.

"Is all good?" Sybille whispered while patting me and I pushed her hand off my shoulder.

"That's wrong Anna. You should have simply listened."

"What's wrong? I still don't understand why he got upset and walked out of the office, can you imagine? After insulting me and putting up a show to humiliate me in front of our other colleagues, so now, you mean, I have to be the one to apologize?"

"And you don't think you should apologize, do you?"

"For what?"

Anna was very opinionated, and explaining to her what she did wrong or suggesting how she could do better would have given me a headache. I hung up, put the phone down and returned to ironing. Anna called my phone many times but I didn't answer.

17

In June, Sybille asked me to pass by her work for a short talk after I dropped off Bernhard at gymnastics training.

She owned a shop that sold presents and offered consultancies for present ideas. It was known as *geschenkideen*. Who needs a consultant before buying a present for someone? One day when I entered her shop, I confirmed that she did it for fun. Who would buy glass balls with some liquid and tiny shining figures inside, colorful small birds made out of papers, stones of different colors and shapes, balls made out of papers that you blow in to form a properly round shape, metal frogs, puppets clothes and shoes and tiny figures made out of wool. "Do you really get clients here?"

"Yes, many. Like last Christmas I run out of stock for some presents," she answered proudly.

"And what do your clients use these things for?" I pointed at some of her products.

"*Geschenk*, a present. What do you use it for?" She mocked me.

"I don't know. I have never received... uhm, received…this kind of present."

I forced myself not to say that I have never received that kind of useless present.

Sybille sipped coffee from a mug resting on her table and started talking. She advised me to register for German class and participate in community activities like her fundraising events. She also suggested that I join the "Afro fam"; it was a group of Africans, descendants of Africa and friends of Africa who lived in the south of Germany. She said it was better than hanging out with the refugees who lived in the camp of Sonnenhof because those ones, she said, would only keep me down and I would never integrate.

"I have nothing against immigrants but you know these people, they are not good for you. Many came in boats or by foot here because their countries have war. They are refugees, not residents like you. Very different, or?" That reminded me of her reaction the day when I invited a Black woman to the house to take down my jumbo braids.

"Do you mean like that woman who I brought home to do my hair?" I had to ask.

"Ah hum, *zum Beispiel*." For example, she answered in German.

"But she is from Nigeria, there is no war there right now."

"Then why would she be here?"

My mouth dropped open. Were refugees only supposed to be from war zones?

Hell might as well freeze over before I would dare to argue with that woman. The discussion would likely have upset her, and I knew she would never understand.

Bernhard, unlike his mother, talked very little. He liked to leave the house when I took him around the park, to Café Felix where he met with his former classmates every Friday morning, to his gymnastics appointments and to watch men who played bowling on the river island Murg. He studied law but had never worked anywhere because his family was wealthy. They had the kind of wealth that assured him he would never miss any of his luxuries like going on holiday every year, attending meditation retreats to reconnect with himself and other things that didn't make sense to me. He had the complete control of his life, and the ability to play with it however it suited him.

On Saturday while we walked in the Kurpark opposite their house, he told me how his parents were not happy with Anna because she refused to take over the family business and left to travel in Latin America.

"Really? Why did she refuse it?"

"She said that she is vegetarian so she can't support meat production. She told papa on the phone that she would rather destroy the butchery than run it. So they sold it to some Turkish guys."

"I didn't know you still have both parents?"

"What do you mean?"

"You know like in my country, many people your age have only their mothers because many men were killed during the Genocide. I don't know why, but I assumed that you only have your mother."

"No, we have both. It's only that our parents divorced when I was 15. We hoped that they would get back together again but now it has been 20 years," he sadly explained.

"And where does your father live?"

"After their divorce he moved into one of our houses in Karlsruhe," he paused to give a sign that I should continue pushing him. "Then shortly after that he moved to the south of France. It's warmer than here in the winter you know." I nodded as if I have been to France and he continued, "He is married and has one child with his French wife. Because of the family business, once in a while he calls or meets with Sybille."

He talked about the places they have been on holiday and about how he used to feel sad because of his disability when he was a teenager, wishing that he could also surf like the others, but ultimately that he accepted that everything happens for a reason and he couldn't fight nature. As a baby, his parents had taken him to different therapies to see if they could fix his legs but nothing worked. He was born in Germany and spent a big part of his childhood in London where they moved when his father got a job as an engineer for a paper producing company. That job inspired him to create Kranz Karton, their family company that recycles papers into packaging cardboards.

Bernhard taught me how to find beauty in everything that nature offered. We would stroll through the park and he explained to me how the leaves of the trees change their colors in autumn. In winter, he would pack a snowball and stick it in my boots, which I would do to him as well, and in summer we went for picnics on island Murg. He spent time painting, creating different arts from handcrafts and whenever I had emotional breakdown, he was there to comfort me. He was to me, like a brother I never had.

18

Facebook and Instagram were platforms where you could meet people you hadn't seen for ages, but not Tendeza. She didn't like social media, even before.

Optimistic she had a change of heart, I created an account on Instagram and called it @tellyourstory_ to stay discrete. Using my real name or posting my photos there could have brought me closer to girls from my neighborhood or family members whom I had never met who would ask me to send them shoes, handbags, perfumes or other things that I couldn't even buy for myself. I checked on people I knew from Kigali who posted photos of their children to see how they were growing up. I checked on my former classmates to find out who broke up with their boyfriend, whose parents died, who got married, places they visited and what they have been eating from Monday until Sunday. That's what people do on social media, right?

Mama Joy was the only person in Rwanda I wrote to on WhatsApp. The guilt of what happened to me after all of her warnings prevented me from telling her much about my life in Germany. I sent her photos from the house, which she said looked like pure heaven on earth. When I showed her the yard, she replied that it looked like the garden of Adam and Eve. For her, everything was always associated with the Bible. One summer night while laying in my room, I called her to hear her voice because I knew it would be full of positivity as always.

"How is Joy doing at school, Aunty?"

"Good, very good. She is finishing primary school this year. She is a smart girl with a brain like yours."

"Thanks Aunty. That's good to hear."

"How is Tendeza? Oh that girl, she arrived in Dubai and now she forgot us poor people, eh?"

"Actually I was about to ask if you have ever heard any news about her. She doesn't contact me, and I have tried every possible way to find her but there is no chance. I am afraid…"

"Oh Jesus, no…she is fine, don't worry. Though recently I told one of my friends from church that you went to live in Europe and your sister is in Dubai and…"

"And what Aunty, oh Mama Joy…" Tears ran down my cheeks before she could finish talking.

"She just said that some young girls die in those Arab countries, or get raped, or get used as housemaids and sometimes end up in prison. You know, all of those kinds of horrible stories…but your sister is fine. Since the day my friend said that, Toni I am telling you, I pray for you and your sister the same as I pray for Joy."

Because finding Tendeza through social media and Mama Joy wasn't working, I started writing her emails hoping that one day, just one day, I would wake up to an answer. Checking my phone whenever it vibrated became a habit, and I would open Gmail and Facebook but there was nothing. Sorrow consumed my days.

"Ma petite Tendeza,

You know what I have learned in this life? There is no wrong or right, different things happen to people and that is okay. We all make mistakes that sometimes hurt or seriously harm others and when money is involved, humans go crazy. I don't know if you have heard, but I also left Rwanda shortly after you. I live in

Germany now. Do you remember those things like people throwing their mobile phones in public trash bins? Like how you could find money on the street in front of supermarkets or train stations? All I have found so far are beggars. Yes, people beg here. Imagine a Muzungu begging. It sounds impossible, right? But they do, I have seen them and one time after school I gave a man one Euro to see if he would accept it, and he did. Afterwards I imagined seeing a headline of a story in the media like "Feeding hungry people in Germany," Mutoni Christine, a Black girl from Rwanda helped a poor white man buy lunch by offering him one Euro. Do you remember what we used to hear about those accessible jobs and fancy dressing nonsense? Forget it. Most people just wear sneakers for the sake of comfort. Anyway, never mind, I just wanted to share some of the things that have surprised me here. I hope you have found happiness and please, write me soon. I love you very much Tendeza, you know that."

19

Two years passed and I learned to differentiate Bratwurst from Weisswurst.

I improved the German I had learned in integration school by becoming active in the community, completed the house chores faster, saved a bit from the allowance Bernhard gave me and made friends including Stefanie, the neighbor who often asked me to help Lukas, her 12 year old son, with English homework.

I learned that Germans always found something to complain about. They complained about bad roads which made me wonder if they have ever seen what a bad road looks like and the weather, even though they still wore jackets in summer "in case it gets windy." I heard complaints about the medical system, the restaurants that had boring menus, the slow public transport, men who talked about German women being boring compared to Latin Americans and the ladies who complained about German men being less charming than the French or Italian men they met on holidays.

Did I mention the food, where they prefer cheap food over quality food? Or the fashion, where they don't dress but simply cover themselves? The most twisted part was the complex insurance system that nobody, at least among the ones I have met, understood.

"In case you need a doctor, medical insurance covers that," Stefanie explained to me after I helped Lukas with his homework.

"Okay," I nodded.

"But if by accident you destroy my window here, which I pray will never happen, there is another insurance that would pay me. I am sure Sybille must have it."

"And if I destroy the window at home?"

"Ouf…I am not sure, but in that case I think it will be your own problem."

"What? So why does that same insurance pay that?"

"It's different. But if for example you destroy the oven or the fridge, there is another insurance."

Lukas saved me from the insurance discussion and asked if we could play a game.

"Sure," I answered, and I followed him into his room.

He wanted us to play the game of guessing colors where one will say the color of something they see and the other had to guess the object.

Lukas started, "*I sehe was, was du nicht siehst und das ist rote.*" I see what you don't see and that is red.

"*Das Auto,*" I said. That was easy to find.

We continued guessing colors and the shock came when Lukas said, "*I sehe was, was du nicht siehst und das ist schwarz.*"

I guessed his table, no. His black car, no. I listed every black object that was in his room, but he kept saying no.

"*Du,*" he said while pointing at me. "*Du bist schwarz.*" You are black. Lukas explained to me that when his mother talks about me with her friends she referred to me that way.

Later when I told Sybille about that game she advised me to stop being too sensitive.

"Lukas is a child. He said simply what he sees," she justified.

"But I found it racist," I said.

"Why is everything becoming racism for you? What's wrong?" Sybille yelled at me.

20

Appreciating my effort to integrate, Sybille allowed me to look for a job, but she refused to hire me when I asked to work in her shop.

She couldn't see how I could advise her clients about the right present to buy and besides, she said, I didn't have the customer service skills required. I searched the internet, sent applications to different companies in the region and waited for their emails, which never arrived or only informed me that they had received my application.

"Is this what you do now that I gave you free time?" She said when she came from the swimming pool and found me in the living room swinging my hips to the left and right with my arms rose high to form the shape of cows horns dancing to the beat of Masamba's song "*Nyeganyega.*"

"But I finished all the work," I answered and switched off the music.

"Why can't you look for *Aussbildung*? To learn something? Life is hard in this country, so you need to work when you are still young otherwise you won't have a pension."

"I studied marketing at university. Maybe I better keep searching for a job in different companies."

"Oh, that reminds me that my friend Claus said he would like to meet you."

"Which one?"

"Do you remember my friend that I told you about. The one with the hotel in Black forest?"

"Yes," I nodded.

"Remind me to give you his contact, he said you should go there for an interview. They are looking for new employees."

The following Monday I went to meet Claus. His office was upstairs at the top of the hotel building with a clear view of the valley Murg. He stood up to shake my hand as I entered and gestured for me to sit in the armchair opposite him. I pulled out my bachelor's degree and laid it on the table carefully to not disturb the other papers that were scattered haphazardly. Claus picked it up and his eyes scanned it for several seconds. Beads of sweat started to rise from my forehead and I had nothing to wipe it off with.

"Do you have a resumé?"

"No, I don't have one," I answered, and he fixed his eyes back on my degree.

"So Mutoni. Tell me about yourself," Claus asked the question I have long feared.

I mumbled a few sentences as hot sweat flowed down my back, soaking the white shirt Sybille had given me for the occasion.

"Can you speak basic German?" Claus asked.

"Yes sir, I have B1 level in German and I can speak enough."

Claus's iPhone vibrated, and he picked it up from the table, "And which kind of job are you looking for?" He asked while reading and responding to his phone messages.

"Any job in my field of education sir, whatever you can offer me in this hotel would be very helpful." Claus didn't answer or lift up his eyes from his iPhone. I watched his fingers scrolling. He sank down in his leather armchair silently and then looked at me.

"*Alles klar,* Mutoni. Let me tell you what I am looking for," he sat up straight and looked into my eyes. "I need a manager for this hotel, a marketing assistant and three *Zimmermädchen.*"

"What is the last one sir?"

"Cleaning ladies for the rooms. So where can you fit yourself?"

"If you give me the opportunity sir, I would love to be a marketing assistant."

Claus stared at me in silence. If a stare could destroy, I would have turned into hundred pieces in that moment.

"Look, I am a good friend of Sybille, I could offer you the cleaning job if you want. Normally I hire people who have experience but I could make an exception in your case."

"But that's what I do the whole time at home sir. I need to practice what I studied."

"Mutoni, I value your degree in marketing but if I can give you some advice, this degree is not going to get you anywhere in this country," he said, lifting up my degree. "There are so many opportunities available for people like you. Why don't you take time and study something that could help you become a nurse, a craftsperson or maybe a driver? The reality is that the type of job you want isn't available for you."

"Thank you for the advice sir, and offering me the cleaning job, but I will keep on searching somewhere else." I stood up to leave. I stifled my tears until I had left Claus's office.

21

It was the best that a summer day could be in the south of Germany. A day so nice that it was hard to believe it could bare bad news. But alas, it did.

My phone rang while I worked in the garden, watching Sybille tan in her deck chair. I cleaned the sweat from my forehead with the back of my palm. My phone buzzed and I pulled it out of my trousers. It was a call from Anna.

"Hey Anna," I said.

She was crying.

"Anna, what's wrong?" I asked.

"Did you read the news?"

"Which news? Where?" I responded, flustered.

"Oh God, I feel so horrible. Maybe it's only in our local newspaper."

"What? Please tell me."

"Sonia died yesterday," she said between gasps.

"Sonia? You mean Sonia, the one who brought me to this country?"

"Yeah, and I feel bad. I blame myself for talking to her. You know…"

"You talked to her? What do you mean?"

"Remember when I called you complaining about my colleague and you got upset?"

"Yes," I said.

"I felt like I owed you an apology, or I had to do something to make your life here better. So, I talked to Tobias about you."

"Your boyfriend?"

"Yes, and your story broke his heart. He agreed that we should report Sebastian and his friends to the police. We had to find Sonia, the only person who could give us the information we needed."

"Uh huh."

"We went to Reeperbahn on Grossefreiheit street and went from one club to another until we found Sonia. She went by her professional name, Soso. Tobias had booked her for an hour. Her boyfriend, who was also her manager, took the money. Tobias explained to him that he wanted to do just a quickie in the car. They joined me in the car which was in the parking lot and then…"

"And then what?"

"I started questioning Sonia. First, she refused to say anything but later as she understood that I had helped you she opened up and began crying. Poor girl. Her life was horrible; it was miserable since she was a teenager in Rwanda. She told me about her family and how they mistreated her. Her father…"

"So, I gave her 50 Euros and thanked her for her time. We watched her walk back and enter the club. Then we drove away."

"So how did she die?" I asked.

"That's what is so sad. This morning I woke up to the article in Hamburger Wochenblatt about her death. She threw herself on the railway of a speeding train three days after we had talked to her."

My heart skipped a beat and I felt a lump forming in my throat. Tears ran down my cheeks as I listened to the rest of the story. Anna told me how the police had a hard time identifying her because her face was smashed. In her apartment, they found her suicide note.

"Dear society, you have failed me but I forgive you. To my family, you gave me a burden too heavy for me to carry. I am sorry.

Sonia Mukamana"

Those were the only words she wrote.

That day my Facebook feed was full of posts from different people. My former classmates posted photos of Sonia, followed by "RIP."

I recalled a memory from when Sonia got pregnant, and the neighbors mocked her that it was from the Holy Spirit. Same as any other Rwandan girl, Sonia grew up going to church. Her father was even a pastor, so on Sundays the whole family always dressed up and went to church where they sang, danced, cried and donated some money for collection.

Her parents made her fear God, the omniscient one who could see everything she did who would punish her by making her burn in hell. The youth in church called her "Umusitari," meaning star, because she was different from most of them. Sonia had a sharp brain, but she also danced hiphop with us at Cente Des Jeunes Kimisagara. Though after, when she arrived home, she was always beaten. Despite this, she still sang along with Whitney Houston whenever her song played on the radio and she still attended church every week.

After high school, as she waited to start university, she had organized youth programs at church, joined groups that took trips to pray in the mountains, and then, all of a sudden, she was pregnant. Teresa, her mother, was humiliated by other Christians and was shamed by her husband that she didn't manage to discipline her daughter according to the word of God. But what could she have done differently? Give her daughter condoms in a society that made conversations about sex between parents and their children a taboo? Advise her to watch out for the pastor's assistant? No, that one was a 'man of God'; the only one, after her father, who had the power to bless or curse others. Her father kicked her out of his house and she moved to live with her Aunty, Teresa's younger sister.

Sonia gave birth at the community health center and named her daughter Umuhoza Denise. She was supported by Mama Joy and my mother, while her father continued living as if she didn't belong to him. She had disobeyed God, so she had to live a shameful life on her own, or so he once told my mother when she tried to make him understand that Sonia needed his support. Nobody ever talked about who Denise's father was.

Unfortunately, at three months old, Denise suffered from pneumonia and died. Sonia's heart broke into pieces. She spent days and nights crying, her mother became desperate until one day someone offered for her to go to Dubai. She needed to get away from her judgmental society, away from sad memories of her daughter, away from Christians who didn't practice what they preached and away from the God who had disappointed her.

22

At the Afro fam, while talking with Patrick about
how to organize the African literature night for the
following month, a soft whisper drifted from
somewhere close behind me. "Hey pretty." Shivering
sensations took over my body. "Hi," I answered, turning
around.

Around me, many were busy exchanging business
cards as they always did at the end of the evening while
others talked about their upcoming projects or
businesses that they had started. I walked towards the
stage to pack the materials I had brought from home for
the presentation about African heroes.

"I am Jan. Jan Bakotesa."

"Nice to meet you Jan. I am Mutoni. How did you
like the evening?" I asked shyly. Maybe my sudden
introversion was because of his eyes, that were as
powerful as a blinding storm.

"Good. What about you?"

"I knew almost everything about the presentation. I helped Patrick to put prepare it when he said that we should discuss Pan Africanism."

"I see. Is Patrick your boyfriend?" Patrick had just left to speak to the lady wearing a purple and green *boubou*.

"No, I don't have a boyfriend. He is from Uganda, so somehow I feel like we are connected. He has a wife here, and two children."

"Come, let's have a drink," he said, and I followed him to the table that had wine and bottles of beer. "Red or white, what do you prefer?"

"Maybe a rosé," I said, settling on the couch with the flyers from earlier in the evening still gripped tightly in my hands.

"Ah *han*, so you like mixing, I see," he teased me while pouring wine into two glasses.

"Cheers," I tipped my glass towards his.

"To what are we cheering?" He asked, tucking back a bunch of hair that had loosened itself from his loose curly bun over the course of the evening.

"To Pan Africanism." I said.

He smiled and raised his glass. "So where are you from, Mutoni?"

"Rwanda. Kigali, specifically."

"I knew it," he screamed. "Lena, come here! I knew it. I was discussing it with my cousin."

"What? You knew what?"

"Just wait a second," he said raising up his hand. Lena joined us. "What is it?" she asked.

"Meet my new friend Mutoni. Guess what!" Jan said.

"What then?" Lena said.

"She is from Rwanda. So I won. Hurry up, give me the ten Euros," he said, gesturing to Lena's handbag.

"What's going on?"

"Didn't you notice how we were staring at you during the presentation when you talked about African heroes?" Lena asked.

"Oh, did you?" I pretended that I didn't see the way they had stared at me, especially Jan.

"Come on," Jan brushed my arm in a flirty way. "It was obvious. Wasn't it?"

"Jan bet that you were from Ethiopia or Rwanda, and I said that you must be from Nigeria or Togo. We said that whoever wins would get ten Euros."

"I see. So you were betting on me?"

"No, no, no wait Lena…let me explain to her correctly. We started talking about how beautiful you are, and I said that such beauty must be from Rwanda or Ethiopia," Jan said.

"Oh, thank you." I wished for the courage to tell Jan how handsome he looked in return, but I wasn't able to let the words escape from my mouth. Life had trained me to become strong and confident, but not eloquent. Lena opened her handbag, took out her wallet, gave Jan ten Euros and returned to the group she had been talking with.

Jan and I talked about everything. We discussed how Germans dress more colorfully during the summer and then turn to black and grey in winter. Jan had visited many European cities, and he liked Paris and Milan, but he thought that he would love Kigali as well if he ever got a chance to travel to Rwanda. Jan's father, Jean Pierre Bakotesa, had moved to Germany from Congo with his German wife, Lisa, who he had met in Goma while she worked for the Red Cross. Jan, a beautiful mixture of both his parents, was born in Hamburg and went to school there until they moved to Gernsbach, where his mother had inherited a house and a restaurant, and his father worked as a journalist for the BT (Badische Tagesblatt). When Jan started university, he moved back to Hamburg and lived in a shared apartment with other students. Later, he returned to work as a coordinator of entertainment events at the SWR3 in Baden-Baden where he lived.

"By the way, may I ask what brought you here? Why Germany?"

"Oh Jan, it's a long, complicated story."

"I love listening to long stories. Of course, only if you want to tell me."

"Hum, maybe another time. Not here."

"Here is my phone number," he handed me his business card. "Just tell me when and where I can listen to your story."

Sybille made a gesture showing me that we had to go. It was getting late.

"Who is that?"

"My mother. We have to go. She is driving and won't like it if I make her wait long."

"I can also drive you home if you want. Gernsbach is on my way."

"That is so kind of you but no, thanks. I am not sure it would be a good idea."

"Are you adopted by her?"

"Jan please, let me answer your questions another day," I said, picking up my bag and jacket.

"Call me anytime." We hugged each other with tenderness as if we had been friends for a long time.

On the way home, Sybille asked me who my new friend was, and I thought of Jan the whole way home. That night I wrote an email to Tendeza.

"Today I met someone.

A special someone. But the thing is, I can't tell if this is wrong or right. His name is Jan. He has awoken in me the same feelings that I felt once as a teenager, but because of mama, I tried hard to silence my heart and it kept me craving for what I never got. It was something I was afraid that I would never have again. Only experiencing small doses of normality didn't work for me, so I left it altogether. You know why? Because our society considered that the right way. A girl was not supposed to have a man in her life, except her father and brother. Well, only after marriage. Jan's eyes have a message for me, I can see it.

This may not be just friendship, it might be something bigger.

What do you think?

I miss you ma petite Tendeza."

23

As I held the bedpan under the bare buttocks of Mrs. Braun, or Frau Braun, as she preferred to be called, I glanced at the clock above the bed as a temporary escape from the strong smell of her urine.

It was exactly 11 o'clock, and that meant it was time for a smoke break, according to my colleague Tess. In order to not appear impatient, I faked a smile and complimented Mrs. Braun's wilting flowers. Her son had brought them last night on his monthly visit. In the two years that I worked there, I had seen many people drop off their parents and never return.

Grey walls and a white ceiling gave the room a depressing atmosphere, despite a beam of sunlight entering through the window. Who is the designer of nursing homes? Do they plan the design around the fact that the lives of its residents are approaching their end? *Die Zeit* newspapers, flowers, fashion magazines and a Rittersport chocolate were scattered on the night table.

The corridor leading to the cleaning room was empty and quiet, except for my footsteps. The cleaning room scared me because it contained a huge sterilizing machine that looked like a monster; a monster that swallowed feces and urine from the patients who were unable to use the toilets. I squeezed the bedpan inside the machine, removed my gloves and washed my hands.

Nneka passed by me, crying and cussing in the corridor. I ran after her trying to ask what was wrong. All I could get as an answer was mutters of, "No, enough is enough." We both ran downstairs as she cried, and I continued asking what was wrong. At the exit of the building, she stopped to wipe her nose with the right corner of her shirt, but I handed her a tissue from my pocket.

"This job, sis, it's not easy," she said sobbing.

"I know Nneka, but is there any alternative for you in this country? And with time you will learn," I said.

Nneka gave me a skeptical look before saying, "There are things I can't learn sis, or that I don't want to learn."

Well, the truth was that, despite my degree in marketing, I never even had a chance to get a better job in Germany before. And when I finally did get an interview, the company wanted a native German speaker. That was clearly not me. After a few attempts and rejections in my field, I followed the path of some of my classmates from an integration course I had taken. Some of them were cleaners and others worked in nursing homes despite their educational backgrounds.

The day I made my decision to work as a caregiver, I called a nursing home in Gaggenau, a city next to Gernsbach and asked if they were looking for employees. The director invited me for an interview the next day. I explained to her what I studied and that apart from taking care of Bernhard, I had no other experience. After a short conversation, she said, "Learning by doing, that's what you will do." That day on the train back home I thought, "Wow, that was so easy." I learned a lot from a job that most Germans would look down upon. My routine remained the same at home, so I had to finish the housework quickly so that I could find time to go to work. I had to remind myself that taking care of the elderly was much better than illegal prostitution which paid mostly in physical abuse. Should I have told Nneka this? Some things are better left untold.

We joined Tess and Effia outside in the garden where they were already smoking. As if each one didn't have their own cigarette or drink, they continued sharing with each other. They all drank from one bottle and passed one cigarette around. I remember once when I asked why they preferred to do it that way, and Effia had answered that this is what strengthened their sisterhood.

"It's a sign of caring, we share what we have."

Oh. yes, I knew about sharing, I thought:

Sharing bacteria,

Sharing poison for the lungs,

Sharing artificial sugar from Coca Cola.

But my opinion would not have counted anyway. Since I didn't smoke, Tess made fun of me and said that I wasn't cool enough for some topics. After all, everyone was free to do whatever she wanted. We promised each other to never judge and always support one another— it was the foundation of our relationship.

I watched the girls as they inhaled and exhaled while I ate a banana. We all looked professional in straight white cotton trousers and matching V-neck company shirts. Nneka exhaled, watched the smoke disappear, then suddenly broke the melancholic silence that had settled. "Guys, can you imagine that Mr. Gizkov grabbed my breast while I dressed him."

We all turned to her and Effia asked, "Who is that?"

"The mushroom-headed old man in room number 110. His sister brought him here last week," Nneka said.

"Ah, you mean Herr Gizkov, the Russian man?" Tess asked.

"No, he is not Russian, Tess. He is German. I saw in his passport that was on the night table next to his bed. And why would you think that Russians come to retire here? " Nneka said. She always fought against tracing people's origins.

"Well, yesterday during the morning shift, one colleague said that we have a Russian patient in room 110. I haven't yet even seen him," Tess explained.

"That's a German thing Tess, for heaven's sake, don't repeat it. They will go back through someone's history who was born here, but whose parents moved here from Turkey 50 years ago, or even longer, and still try to call that person Turkish," Nneka said.

Effia kept smoking indifferently as if she wasn't part of the conversation.

Before Nneka and Tess started fighting about the ethics of digging into people's roots, I had to step in between them. Tess was still new in Germany; it was our duty to explain her that being a descendant of a different nationality doesn't define your identity.

I had to make her understand that probably, Herr Gizkov, had suffered enough trying to answer where he came from. And he was not the only one.

"You know what Tess, we are all immigrants from somewhere. When we leave this world, nobody will take their nationality to the grave with them," I said.

"I know. It's not like I am discriminating or something," Tess said. We all looked at each other in silence.

The first time I met Tess was at work in the dressing room. She turned to leave after changing out of her work uniform and saw me opening my wardrobe behind her.

"Your hair looks weird," she said.

"Excuse me, what did you say?" I turned to her.

"Nothing bad. It's just that your hair looks like you got an electric shock. The way it's standing messily."

I moved closer to her and asked her to touch my Afro, which I always had to cover with a cap or wear in cornrows during work. She touched it.

"It feels like normal hair, doesn't it?" I asked.

"Uhmm…it feels like a wool somehow. Is there any way that you can fix it?"

I thought she was out of her mind, but in the following days she wanted to be close to me and asked many questions, and I realized that she was simply ignorant of other skin colors, races and cultures.

To resolve the fight with Nneka on nationality, I had to make her understand, that for example, no amount of skin bleaching will turn a person of color into a white European. Never.

"Are you guys talking about me?" Effia asked.

"Come on, your skin is naturally lighter. Isn't it? But look for example at Alice, that girl from Burundi," Nneka said.

"The one who likes to work weekend shifts?" Effia asked.

"Yes, that one, she thinks she is a real *oyibo*. I knew her when she had just arrived here, and her skin was as dark as yours Toni, I swear."

"Jealousy will kill you. Isn't it her own skin? It would be an issue if she was bleaching yours," Effia said, pushing Nneka on the shoulder. Tess and I laughed.

"No, that's not the problem," Nneka said while giggling.

"What's wrong then?"

"Try to talk to her in Kirundi or Swahili and you will see. That woman, hum, she only forces herself to speak Deutsch."

"Do you speak Swahili, Nneka? How do you know she won't respond to you?" I asked.

"Of course, I speak the basic of *habari gani, asante sana, hakuna matata, jina lako ni nani.*"

"Wow, that is already a lot," Tess said.

"Anyway, back to you Tess. Let me tell you something as a sister, okay? Even after you speak German like a native and denounce your Filipino nationality to get a German passport, you will never be considered a German by this society. It has been fifteen years since I moved here and I am German by law, but I am always seen as an outsider," Effia said.

"Preach mama, preach," Nneka said with her thumbs up. It was a sign that she often made instead of saying, "It is clear enough. Now stop."

"By the way Mutoni, how did you come here?" Nneka asked me.

"With the tram S81."

Effia and Tess giggled.

"Come on, I mean here in this country."

"With an airplane. Didn't we all fly here?" I said and laughed, gesturing to the others.

"What made you leave Rwanda? As far as I know, Effia came to hunt for money, Tess and me, we were brought by love."

"Brought by love, really?" Effia asked mockingly.

"Agh girls, it's a long story. We shall talk about it when Effia invites us all out."

We all laughed because Effia saved all of her money and sent most of it home to Uganda every month.

24

Maritess "Tess" Nacario (from Philippines), 22 years old

Tess came to Germany one year after getting married to Volker Schmitt, a 60-year-old man who she met while he was in Manila on work missions for the German Development Aid. He needed someone who would take care of him once he retired. He had met Tess at his hotel in Manila where she worked as a room cleaner after dropping out of school to make some money and support her mother to raise her younger siblings. Volker had promised Tess that she would go back to school in Germany and he would support her family financially, but when they arrived he didn't keep his promises.

Nneka Grace (from Enugu, Nigeria), 25 years old

Nneka is an actress and singer. She married Lucas, a German man she had met on an online mixed-race dating website.

Lucas had made Nneka believe that Germany was the 'Promised Land' that the Holy Bible talks about. While dating, he sent her clothes from Kik and New Yorker, and cosmetics that didn't match her skin tone but Nneka loved them anyway because they were from Europe. When she told us her story, I imagined that she must have looked like a zebra when she put that foundation and concealer on her skin. Nneka is black. Not dark skin but Black. Lucas traveled to meet Nneka's family and they were married in Nigeria. It was a big and fancy wedding, Nneka said.

Once in Germany, Nneka discovered that her husband drank from Monday to Sunday, was frequently absent the whole day and when he returned home, he beat her. She ran away and moved to Leipzig where she had a cousin who she heard from her mother, was a medical doctor married to a German woman. She lived with her cousin for five months, which were difficult for his wife to handle. To avoid troubles in her cousin's marriage, Nneka went to the women's shelter in Karlsruhe where someone had told her that people were more friendly than in Leipzig. People at the women's shelter listened to her story, gave her a room, donated some clothes and food and helped her to get papers.

Later she moved to Gernsbach. Nneka has been living in Germany for 10 years.

Effia Mirembe (from Uganda), 35 years old

Effia is a nurse who spent all of her savings coming to Europe. She had been told that nurses were highly needed and paid very well in Germany. After six months of hiding from the police to avoid deportation, she managed to find Olgun who agreed to marry her under one condition: she would give him 50 percent of her salary for three years.

At first, Effia worked only 20 hours per week and combined it with attending German classes. Slowly, she realized that her salary was nothing compared to her expenses. She stopped classes and started working full time and taking extra shifts. Olgun's family had moved from Turkey to Germany when he was five years old and he doesn't have any memory of his life in Turkey. For him, Germany is home, despite the fact that he is always called Turkish. After five years, Effia divorced Olgun and married Semakula, a Ugandan guy that she had known in school. When Semakula arrived in

Germany, he became like a five-year old boy trapped in the body of a grown man who never wanted to do anything at home, while Effia worked to bring money. For him, a man was not supposed to clean or cook. But Effia remained kind and patient with him. Effia spoke very little, listened attentively and helped all of us with whatever we didn't know at work.

I have worked with these three women for two years. The two years were spent desperately clinging to the hope that one day we may get promoted to a higher position where we wouldn't have to change diapers, wash wounds or struggle lifting patients. However, whenever they asked me about my immigration journey, I always found a way to dodge the conversation.

I crawled into bed every night, feeling ready to collapse at the end of the day. My job at the nursing home was very demanding. I wondered if the world was truly as cold as I viewed it. Nobody was there for me. There was nobody to listen to my prayers that I whispered between sobs in the dark during night while Sybille and Bernhard slept comfortably upstairs. The nights were long as I ruminated about my job and the hopelessness of finding my sister.

When Sybille realized that I was struggling mentally, she booked me an appointment at talk therapy. The psychotherapist was a friendly woman who, I was sure, was the best in the region. However, when I arrived, I was greeted by a white German, born in Freiburg, who studied in Switzerland and London and then returned to work in Karlsruhe. I didn't say much during the session. How could she understand what I was suffering from? In that moment, I wished for someone with an immigrant background and even better, a person of color. But such a psychotherapist was not available in our region.

We created our own sort of therapy union at work. If one of us felt like their heart was becoming heavy, they would share their emotional struggles and we were always there to listen and offer support. That was something I didn't find in Afro fam. There, we only talked about how to promote African art and architecture, organized educational seminars, attended

workshops about cultural exchange and represented
Africans living in Germany.

25

In Germany, categorizing the financial status of people based on their physical appearance is as hard as putting on underpants by pulling it over the head.

At least this is how I used to think, until I met the fish vendor at the farmers market who proved me wrong. I loved to walk through colorful fruits and vegetables, and choose what I wanted without vendors shouting to me like markets in Rwanda where vendors would run after you, yelling, "Sister buy from me, sister good bananas, sister *maracuja*." The downside was that in Germany, though the fruits looked clean and polished, they were tasteless. Sybille knew that I loved going to the market, so every Friday we would go together. That day she had an appointment at the dentist, so I went alone.

When it was my turn to get served at the fish truck, I asked how many grams a piece of trout fish (*Forelle*) weighed. Instead of answering my question, the vendor raised his eyebrows and said, "*Das kostet aber Geld.*" But this costs money.

The vendor threw together three pieces of leftovers from other different types of fish that he had sold and tried to make me an unprofessional, cheap offer. The leftover pieces looked like tails from maybe Trout, Tylapia, Mackerel…and something else I was not interested in knowing. He said, *"Schau Mal, die drei Stueckchen hier sind billiger. Wills du die vielleicht nehmen?"* Look, the three small pieces here are cheaper, do you maybe want to take them?

Instinctively, I tightened my mouth, and breathed in and out to calm myself down. This helped me to stop my tongue from expressing the anger that was starting to boil in my brain. I gathered myself and managed to change my order. I asked the weight of a piece of Salmon steak (*Lachsfilet*) that was next to the one I tried to order before. His answer was worse than the first! *"Ohh…Lachs ist aber teuerer, willst du es kaufen?"* Salmon is more expensive; do you want to buy it?

"Jesus…Can't you just answer my question?" I thought. Assuming that I grew up with better discipline, I replied with a clear *"Ja bitte."* Yes please.

Was he very kind and wanted a poor woman to save her money? Or was he used to Black people in our region being poor refugees? Was he not understanding my question even though I spoke his mother tongue?

He put the little leftover tails on his scale, told me the weight and started to explain to me, again, how they are from very good fish, fresh from the sea and much cheaper than the others that I had wanted to order. There was an old couple standing next to me waiting to be served by the colleague of my dear fish vendor. The couple had been following the discussion and glanced at me nervously from time to time, but remained silent. The man's cheap offer was getting on my nerves and I couldn't hold it in anymore. I have had enough of that kind of behavior.

So I asked him: "*Wissen Sie, ob ich Geld habe oder nicht? Wo haben Sie gelesen, dass ich günstiger Fish kaufen soll? Ich weiss genau was ich kaufen möchte, und das sind nicht die Reste von den Schwänzen.*" Do you know if I have money or not? Where did you read that I should buy cheaper fish? I know exactly what I want and that is not the leftover tails.

The vendor's colleague and the old couple looked embarrassed! Shame appeared on the vendor's face. It was the kind of shame that made it apparent that he wished his fish truck could swallow him! Finally, I got my original order and left feeling satisfied.

While I have faced challenges, many of my neighbors were helpful and smiled to me when we met on the road. Gernsbach was small enough for me to recognize many familiar faces and its mountains and forests made me feel safe. Or maybe my sense of security was because I knew that I was far away from Hamburg, the city that had traumatized me.

There were moments when I felt a sense of community. Like one evening a drunken man yelled at me at the tram station. I didn't understand what he was saying so I kept walking, afraid he might become aggressive. I heard an old woman across the road yell that she would call the police if he dared to say such things one more time. The women from the community library always recommended me helpful books I could borrow. Somehow, I started to understand what my friend Fabiola from Afro fam had once told me. She had said that if I kept seeing myself as a problem in the community, I would become one because my thoughts had the power to lead my life. Fabiola had advised me that since I couldn't change the way that society treated me, I could at least have to change the way it affected me. Fabiola moved to Germany from Columbia when she was ten years old and studied Mathematics. A few years after finishing university, Fabiola experienced that she couldn't get a job as a Mathematics teacher because of her strong Spanish accent. She worked as a German-Spanish translator at the integration center of Stuttgart.

26

Jan put his arm around my shoulder and an electric current moved through my whole body. We walked slowly in the Kurpark next to each other and watched the ducks swimming in the small river.

"Toni, I want to know you more."

"What do you want to know? Ask me."

"Like that long story you have avoided telling me, for example."

"Do you really want to hear this, Jan?"

"Yes, I do. Please why do you keep me begging?"

"Alright." We sat on a bench and i laid my head against his shoulder. I told him my story. The whole story. I started from the day I arrived in Hamburg city. I talked about the men who raped me in Blankenese. I told him about Sebastian's physical abuse, and how Anna brought me to Gernsbach. Jan listened carefully, stroking my back gently and squeezing my shoulders from time to time. I didn't shift from my seat, I didn't raise my voice or cry loudly, but tears ran down my cheeks as I spoke. When my story came to an end, Jan hugged me tight and held my face with both hands so that he could look properly into my eyes.

"You are brave," he said, kissing my forehead. I said nothing, and self-consciously cleaned my face, feeling embarrassed and worried that he knew the darkest parts of my life.

Jan watched me in silence and his stare made me shy.

"I like watching you. Have you noticed that?"

"Yes, I did. Starting from the first time you saw me at the Afro fam event."

"Exactly. I feel like people around here in general don't like to be watched, but how can we truly get to know each other then?"

"I don't know, maybe we can ask what we want to know."

"Words are not enough to capture people. Every human has their own energy. You have a special energy, a nice one."

Suddenly shy, I looked away. "Is this all you have to say in response to my story?"

"No, that is what I see in your eyes. Let's walk back to your house."

Jan held my hand as we walked. We were talking about the weather, commenting on the leaves that were turning yellow and red, when all of a sudden, he stopped in front of me, blocking the way, and looked in my eyes. "Toni, may I tell you something?"

"Sure," I said.

Fear grew inside me and I felt sad thinking that it could be the last time I saw Jan.

At school, I once read a story of Tess of the d'Ubrevilles who, after marriage, told her husband about how she was raped and he decided to abandon her. But then I consoled myself that I was planning to leave Germany anyway. How could I lose him when he wasn't mine? We were just friends.

"Toni," he inhaled deeply, and exhaled slowly.

"What is it Jan? Say it."

"You have no idea how beautiful you are."

I blushed and walked past him, unsure of how to respond. We continued talking about his winter projects and his planned holidays to Spain. When we arrived at my house, he kissed me goodbye on the lips. I trembled with feeling and my lips wanted more, but he entered his car and drove away.

In the days that followed we became inseparable. He was already waiting in the parking lot for me when I finished work. He accompanied me and Bernhard to play Boule on Murginsel and invited me to concerts he had organized. Whenever my phone vibrated, I knew that he had sent me a message or a photo. We chatted on WhatsApp whenever we weren't together.

"My dear Tendeza,

Why don't you answer any of my emails? I am confused and I worry everyday. If you are still upset and simply don't want to communicate with me at least let me know that you are fine.

Have I ever told you what mama said that day when she slapped me because she had seen me holding hands with Abdoul on our way from the market? She told me to stay away from boys because they bring only pain and suffering in women's lives. Do you believe that? Today Jan kissed me. It was a short version of that kind of kiss we used to see in movies. By the way, I am going back home soon but Kigali won't feel like home without you. I have saved enough money to start a business so please come and we shall work together. My ability to hold on to this life has become as slow as a snail crossing the road.

I am sending you hugs."

27

Nobody leaves Europe to return to the dust and mosquitoes of Africa unless they are deported by force. Nneka had told me one evening while we emptied the trash bins after preparing the patients for bed.

I had just told her that I had submitted my resignation letter and the supervisor said that I would have to work an additional three months and after that, I was free to leave. Nneka was supposed to keep it a secret and I planned to tell Effia and Tess about it myself on the weekend. But Nneka wasn't able to keep it a secret for even one night.

"So, you are tired of boots and coats in winter? Or is it because of your experience at work? You are doing a very good job. Much better than most of us."

"No. It has nothing to do with work," I answered.

Nneka was referring to my frequent complaints about the patients, who, at 6:30 in the morning as I woke them up with a warm, "Good morning", greeted me in return with, *"Schwester, wo kommst du denn her*?" Where are you from? Of course, I wished they could have said something like, "Thanks for being here for us" or simply, "Good morning."

"But Toni, you live with a rich family; I can imagine you don't need this job anymore."

"It's not just the job Nneka, I will go back home as I told you. In five months I will return to Rwanda."

"Look at you, acting serious," she teasingly pushed my shoulder.

"I am serious. I am going home to tell people about the real life in Europe."

"And you think they will listen to you and believe what you say?" Nneka said mockingly.

"Well, if they refuse to listen then I will write a book and hopefully someone will read it."

"Oh by the way, you know, when I came to your house that day, oh my God, I wasn't sure I could allow myself to step on that spotless floor. Luckily your madam invited me in the living room, and I looked everywhere as if I was coming from the bush," she shook her head. "Very rich people." She put a new trash bag in her container, "Spoiled woman…so now you are tired of paradise, eh. Aren't you?"

"That's not my family Nneka, you know well how I live there," I said while washing my hands.

"But you are allowed to live there. Is that not a big luxury?"

"Look, everything sucks here. There is no place for me in this society, I don't belong here, and I know somewhere where life is different. What is the use of fighting for something that you were told is the best life when it means losing everything that you are?"

"Oh really, everything sucks? It's so horrible to have electricity 24/7. It sucks to have water running always plus a hot shower if you fancy it. It is horrible to walk on clean streets without any mud or dust. It sucks to live in a society where everyone has a medical insurance, a roof over their head and you can eat whatever you want without any worry. Is this what you mean sucks?" Nneka was becoming upset.

"Please Nneka, just leave that topic alone."

"Why can't you focus on the positive side, Toni?"

"Maybe we are different."

"That is obvious."

We walked to the dressing room without talking to each other. She changed from her work uniform to her clothes. I put on my jeans and sneakers and we walked out of the nursing home, an uncomfortable silence settling around us.

In the parking lot she turned to me, "Is it maybe because of last time at the club? The other story you told us about when you were out with your half-caste boyfriend."

"His name is Jan."

"Oh yeah, Jan. A very German name for a half-caste guy."

"Half-caste is like an insult Nneka. Please, I hope you will never say it when he is around."

"So, is that the reason you are leaving?"

"No, that's nothing. The guy at the door of the club was just flexing his power," I said as we walked to the tram station.

Nneka meant when I went to the club with Jan a few months ago, and the security on the door refused us entry. We queued like others and people were moving inside the club one after another, but when Jan walked to enter, the security guard pushed him backward with his palm. "*Ihr dürft nicht rein,*" he said. You are not allowed inside. The security guard told us that our Afro hair was too messy for their club. Jan asked if he could talk to the manager but the security guard refused. I could see how Jan's anger was rising. He held my hand to leave and shouted that we will never go to their club and that we would report him to the management.

28

Tess and Effia already knew about my plan to go back home. Tess wanted to keep my shoes, the only ones that I was planning to leave behind. She used to tease me that I was addicted to sneakers. Effia had suggested that she would host a goodbye party for me, but added in typical Effia fashion that I could invite a maximum of twenty guests.

"We came here to stay sis. No going back to Africa," Nneka said while we served ourselves from the Asian buffet. Tess had invited us for lunch at *Alles inklusive Mongolei*, an Asian restaurant in Karlsruhe that offered a buffet plus drinks and ice cream for only seven euros.

"There are problems I need to solve back home, Nneka."

"Problems of land or did you also leave a kid there like Effia?" Tess asked.

"No, I don't have a child. It's just a personal issue."

"Do we have secrets?" Nneka asked while pointing at me, then back to Tess and Effia. " Since when do we keep secrets from each other? Aren't we sisters?"

"Maybe she has one of those rich African men putting pressure on her to return home. Just leave her alone," Tess said.

We filled our plates, grabbed Coca Cola and then went to sit. We talked about different things as we ate.

"When I came to this country, everything was exciting. Each year I planned how I would go home to visit, but I didn't go. Compared to all of you, I was lucky to immediately find a job, maybe because I am a nurse. I send money home every month but I don't get the courage to fly there. Somehow, I feel like I have nothing to take back there except shame and failure," Effia said.

"Why shame, Effia?"

"You know the picture that people back home create in their minds when they know that you live in Europe?" Effia said.

"Yes, like the picture Alice shows them on social media," Nneka answered.

"Agh, you and that Burundian, it is like you are always in competition to impress your followers," Tess said.

"But seriously," Nneka put her fork down and reached into her handbag to bring out her phone. "Look at her Instagram photos, you would think she is a big boss lady somewhere who owns a business." She swiped left showing us some photos.

"So now show us yours, and then we will see the difference," Effia said.

"But no comments, okay?" She showed us some photos in the middle of the street, surrounded by cars parked on the roadside, at the swimming pool, in shopping malls and many others.

"You are both young and beautiful. That is what I can see," Effia said.

"This is exactly the kind of thing I knew you would say," Nneka responded.

"By the way, Toni, I didn't ask if you are leaving with German nationality?" Tess asked.

"No, I didn't apply for it. I knew from the beginning somehow that I preferred one day to return home."

"But you could still return there as a German," Nneka said.

"I prefer to return there as a Rwandan."

"Can't you be both?" Tess asked.

"No, unfortunately. I remember when I went through the process for my application, they asked me to denounce my Ugandan nationality," Effia explained.

"You know when I get my papers," Tess paused, "I'll show my husband the stripes under my sneakers." She lifted up the soles of her shoes to demonstrate.

"But you have papers, Tess. You have a residence permit," I said.

"No, not that one. Once I become German and I am holding my German passport in my hands, I will find a reason to divorce him and can get myself someone like that," she pointed at a guy around 20 years old wearing jeans so tight it made me wonder how he let his farts out.

"Ah okay. Me? I'll go for a rich old man about to die. Rich and old…so he can leave me with his property," Nneka said.

They laughed, but I didn't.

We finished eating and went to walk around the city. Whenever we passed by fancy buildings, Nneka stopped to take a selfie. We discussed about who to invite to my goodbye party and delegated tasks. Nneka would cook jollof rice and help Effia to clean up the kitchen after the party. Tess said that she would make salad and spring rolls and would also help to clean up the living room. I also needed to tell Jan to invite his friends. Since it was my party, I didn't have to worry about food or drinks. Effia would take care of the music for dancing, decorations and drinks. On top of that, she would make fried chicken and a sauce to go with Nneka's jollof rice. If I wanted, Effia said, I could make chapatti.

29

While we ate breakfast, I told Sybille and Bernhard that I had decided to leave Germany.

"Are you not happy living with us?" Sybille asked.

"What can we do to make your life better here?" Bernhard asked.

"I can arrange a sleeping room for you here upstairs with us. Would leaving the basement make you happy?" Sybille asked.

"That is very kind, but thanks. I am happy with everything and I will always be grateful that you welcomed me into your family and taught me to become the woman I am today."

"What's wrong then? I don't understand why you are leaving," Sybille said.

"I have three different lives, and I don't fully fit into any of them. Hanging out with my colleagues is good and fun, but they sometimes treat me as an outsider because I live in a rich white family. I know, I have a lot of privilege compared to them. And here at home, none of you understand my experiences in this country, which is largely shaped by the color of my skin. That's something I cannot change. In Afro fam, I hang out with multicultural architects, doctors and successful artists but as soon as I leave, I realize that I don't fit in there."

"And that is why you are leaving?" Bernhard asked.

"More or less, yes, that is why."

"Will your life in Rwanda be different than before?" Sybille asked.

"Oh yes, it will be better. I grew up, I learned a lot about life, I am able to fight for what I want, and I will become a business owner."

"Which business?" Bernhard asked.

"I plan to open a smoothie bar where I will make and sell juice and smoothies from fresh fruits. My idea will be to buy fruits directly from the farmers and when the business grows, I want to employ single mothers from my community."

"And what does Jan say about it?" Bernhard asked.

"He doesn't know yet. I haven't told him."

"He is a cool guy." Bernhard cleared his throat, "We don't talk much but I can see that he cares about you."

Sybille pushed her plate to the side and stood up, "Okay, I will talk to the lawyer about how to proceed with the divorce. I will also call Anna to tell her this sad news."

"It's not like I will be gone forever, I will come back to visit you for sure. You are also welcome to visit me. Bernhard, you will love my country, trust me."

Before bed I sent another email to my sister.

"Dear Tendeza,

I am confused and I worry everyday about you. What happened? As I wrote you last time, I am going back home. I already bought my ticket for Wednesday night. Europe, my dear, is shockingly different from the pictures and movies we have seen. My life here has been an adventure full of ups and downs. I hope to tell you all the details one day in this life. I love you and I miss you."

30

The day Effia had told me about finally arrived.

My feet had become swollen and pain radiated from every part of my back. There was only one week left before I finished my last three months and I decided to push through without taking a sick leave. Winter was falling and most of our colleagues became sick, which meant work hours increased. Instead of taking care of eleven people in one shift of six hours, I had to take care of fifteen or more.

"You don't have to do this. Just tell your supervisor you can't do it anymore," Jan told me one evening while he massaged my feet. He had come to visit after work.

"I need the money Jan. Besides, I only have a week left, and I won't have to work there anymore. I have already resigned."

"I am happy about your decision. I could talk to my parents if you want to work a few hours in a restaurant?"

"No, I can't."

"It's good also to rest. You know what," he put my foot on the bed and turned to me, suddenly excited. "Now you could come with me to Spain since you will have no job. It will be fun, I promise."

"When is that?"

"I booked the flight for December, shortly before Christmas."

"Let's see. I am not sure."

We ate pizza and drank beer he had brought. He laid on his stomach next to me. "Toni."

"Yes," I turned to look into his eyes.

"How was it growing up in Kigali?"

"It was good. Very good."

"Yeah, but good how? Give me details like your neighborhood, friends, school or your hobbies."

I shifted on my side to face him. "My neighborhood where I was born and grew up in is called

Nyamirambo." Jan tried to repeat it, "Namirabo." I laughed before correcting him, "No, Nya-mi-ram-bo."

"Okay, I will practice."

"In general, the neighborhood was Muslim, but there were also a few Christians. "We always played ball on the street, sometimes on the way from school or if we were sent to go to the market. My mother owned a small restaurant that made the best food in the hood," I giggled.

"And how are the people?"

"Very warm and friendly. But if you want to buy something you have to be ready to bargain, for example, and some people are not good at that. I grew up eating fresh fruits from the neighbors. Fruits that have a real taste, you cannot compare them with the fruits from here."

"That sounds interesting. I would like to visit Kigali one day," he caressed my cheek softly in silence.

"Jan," I paused. He stopped touching me.

"I am sorry I touched you. I promise to never do anything you don't like," he said.

"No, I enjoyed it. It was good."

We both stared at the painting that Bernhard had given me that was hanging on the wall close to the entrance.

"I like your room. It's cozy."

"Jan, can you stay here tonight?" I said abruptly.

Our eyes met and I knew we were both feeling the same hot sensations, and with the flash of an anxious silence, he pulled me closer. Ecstasy filled my heart and I could read the same in his eyes. We made love and for the first time in my life, I experienced flying to the edge of the world and landing on a very bouncy trampoline. We spent the whole night cuddling.

31

The party looked like an African festival.

Different food was arranged around Effia's living room and people mulled about everywhere, serving themselves.

Despite horrible weather, everyone who was invited came. People dressed colorfully because Effia had said it that was the dress code. We ate as much as we could from fried plantain, rice and isombe to chapatti, spring rolls and salad. We danced, swinging our hips up and down until our feet started hurting. Semakula, Effia's husband, had selected songs from Sauti Sol, Eddy Kenzo, and Makanyaga. I called Mama Joy on video so that she could see how the party was. But because she had always wanted to visit my home in Germany, I didn't want to kill her excitement by telling her that it was actually my goodbye party.

Jan had come with two of his colleagues, however, he was still mad at me.

Finding the words to explain to him that I was leaving Germany for good was impossible for me whenever we met, so I sent him a WhatsApp message the night before the party with the exact date of my departure. He had replied to that message with a simple, "Let's talk about this." As we slowly got tired of dancing, we went to stand in the kitchen.

"Toni, I need to know why you are leaving for good."

"Why? I am going home."

"This can also be your home. Please tell me your reason, if I deserve to know."

"I am tired of everything here Jan, I need a break."

"So what about me?" His sad eyes were full of strong trying to exude strength, even though I was dying inside.

"I love you, Toni. I thought you must have seen it but apparently you don't even care at all."

Our lips moved closer in a blink of an eye and we kissed passionately.

"I need to leave Jan, I know that I will miss you so much but your special place in my heart will remain yours and my lips will wait for you."

"What is taking you away from me?" He asked, holding both of my hands on his face.

"Do you have any idea what it is like to live in a society that doesn't trust you? Can you imagine what it is like to be refused opportunities or treated with little respect because of your skin color, something you can not change? Have you ever had to leave your home because it's your only choice and you ended up in a place where people clearly see you as a problem?" I cried, laying my head on his chest. He caressed my cheeks and kissed my forehead.

"It's fine, my love, you can cry as long as you want. I am here."

"Don't get it wrong," I said between sobs, "That's not why I am leaving. Otherwise it would be letting prejudice win. I saved enough money over the last five years and I acquired skills that I am going to use to build the life I want in Rwanda. At some point in life everything comes to the end, and I feel that this is the end of my time in Germany."

Effia entered the kitchen and when she saw us, suggested that we could talk freely in her bedroom, but Jan said that it was better for us to leave the party. I went in the living room to tell Bernhard and some other friends that I was leaving.

We drove to Jan's apartment, where he took care of me and made sure I rested enough. His bed, smelling strongly of him, made me fall asleep quickly. I slept deeply, as I have not slept for a long time. In the morning, I woke up to the smell of fresh croissants. Jan had left me sleeping to prepare breakfast on a small table in his kitchen. I sat with a view of the Leopold Platz in the center of Baden-Baden, but I wasn't interested in looking outside. Instead I watched Jan, the guy who was showering me with love and I felt sad knowing that in one week I was moving far away from him.

32

On Monday around noon, Tess and Nneka came home to pick up the things that I had told them I would not take with me.

Sybille had cooked *Maultasche* with minced meat sauce. In my last week, she was very friendly, and I also wanted to show her my gratitude in return. We ate lunch all together; laughing at anything that was said, knowing it would likely be the last time we would laugh together like that. Our neighbor Stefanie had brought an orange cake for desert.

While we cleaned up the table, Sybille asked me to talk to Anna who had said she would call during her lunch break.

"Yes, I am fine. Yeah, I am ready to leave," I said on the phone. She thanked me for everything and apologized for any times that she had done or said something inappropriate. Emotional, I responded that I should be the one thanking her for saving my life and giving me a family. She was also sorry that she didn't manage to come and say goodbye in person. I walked Tess and Nneka to the tram station and hugged them goodbye, not even harboring the tiniest hope that they would come to visit me in Rwanda.

Afterwards, I went to Sparkasse bank and withdrew all of my money. They advised me to complete an online bank transfer to my Rwandan account once it was created, but I wanted to return home with the money in my hands. I carried a backpack full of thirty thousand euros home and spread it in my suitcase.

Wednesday night was my flight from Frankfurt airport. While I packed the last remaining items in my hand luggage, Bernhard brought me a portrait of myself that he had been painting since the day I told them that I was leaving. "I will send you my selfie with the gorillas when I visit them," I said teasingly. Sybille drove me to Karlsruhe train station. She hugged me goodbye and gave me an envelope, which I later realized had five hundred euros. Jan called me while I was in the train to Frankfurt airport to wish me a safe journey. He couldn't make it to the airport because he had an important meeting at work.

In the airport, I checked in and dropped off my suitcase. While walking to find my departure gate, I felt proud of myself for the first time in my life. I have learned a new language, made money and friends and experienced life in ways I couldn't have imagined before.

A hand tapped me on the shoulder, "Hey pretty, what are you running away from?" The voice sounded familiar and I turned around immediately.

"Jan!" I screamed, "What are you doing here?" I jumped up into his arms, full of joy and confusion.

"Don't you remember I told you that I would like to visit Kigali one day," he said, looking in my eyes which were filling with tears. He kissed my hand and added, "Let's go to the gate."

Acknowledgments

I would like to thank my editor Leah Dunlevy for dedicating her time and creativity to this book.

Special thanks to Hope Azeda for allowing me to grow up in Mashirika, to Jean de Dieu Uwihanganye for seeing a writer in me before I could even believe in myself, to Sam Kyagambidwa and the writers of Urunana soap opera for taking me under their wings.

To Christina Pauls, Fanny Kranz, Jackie Kanda, Kerstin Qwuarch-Probst and Cadeau Mbabazi who really understood this story and supported me in different ways. *Vielen Dank.*

I am grateful to family Strauß, Sarah and Roman Schuler, Diane Kamali, Florian Arnold for their support and encouragement, many kind people in my extended family and acquaintances whose stories and characters inspired this novel.

To the sisters that art gave me, Eliane Umuhire, Clementine Dusabejambo, Denyse Umuhuza, Shanel Nirere and Jemima Kakizi. Thank you for empowering me to keep moving forward by simply being part of my creative life. *Ndabakunda.*

Lastly but most importantly, thanks to my loved ones for their love , encouragement and the ability to tolerate my mood and absence.